GULLIVER'S TRAVELS

The Politics of Satire

TWAYNE'S MASTERWORK STUDIES

Robert Lecker, General Editor

GULLIVER'S TRAVELS

The Politics of Satire

Ronald Knowles

TWAYNE PUBLISHERS
An Imprint of Simon & Schuster Macmillan
New York

Prentice Hall International
London • Mexico City • New Delhi • Singapore • Sydney • Toronto

Twayne's Masterwork Studies No. 158

Gulliver's Travels: The Politics of Satire
Ronald Knowles

Twayne Publishers
An Imprint of Simon & Schuster Macmillan
1633 Broadway
New York, New York 10019

Library of Congress Cataloging-in-Publication Data

Knowles, Ronald, 1940–
     Gulliver's travels : the politics of satire / Ronald Knowles.
         p.   cm. — (Masterwork studies : no. 158)
     Includes bibliographical references (p.).
     ISBN 0-8057-4617-X (cloth). — ISBN 0-8057-4618-8 (paper)
         1. Swift, Jonathan, 166■■■■■■■■■■■■■■ 2. Politics and literature—
     Great Britain—History—18th century.   3. Political satire, English—History and
     criticism.   4. Voyages, imaginary, in literature.   I. Title.   II. Series : Twayne's
     masterworks studies ; no. ; 158.
     PR3724.G8K66   1996
     823'.5—dc20   95-46869
                                                                                                                CIP

109876543   (hc)
1098765432   (pb)

Printed in the United States of America

To Howard Erskine-Hill

Contents

Note on the References
and Acknowledgments

Paul Turner's current World's Classics edition of *Gulliver's Travels* (Oxford: Oxford University Press, 1986) reproduces early typography, contains valuable notes, and is generally available. It is referred to throughout this study by page number, preceded by that of part and chapter in Roman numerals (as in I.ii.23) to facilitate reference for those using other editions. Other references to Swift are to the *Prose Works of Jonathan Swift*, edited by Herbert Davies (fourteen volumes, Oxford, Basil Blackwell, 1939–68), referred to in the text as *Prose Works*. Quotation of Swift's letters are from *The Correspondence of Jonathan Swift*, edited by Sir Harold Williams (five volumes, Oxford, Clarendon, 1963–65), referred to in the text as *Correspondence*. Chambers Harrap Publishers, Ltd., are thanked for permission to reproduce the illustrations by Willy Pogány from *Gulliver's Travels* (London, 1919).

I owe a debt of thanks to my Swift students over many years at the University of Reading, but the deepest gratitude is to my first teacher on the eighteenth century, to whom this study is dedicated.

Jonathan Swift. Engraving by Edward Scriven, 1818, after the portrait
by Francis Bindon, 1738.

Chronology:
Jonathan Swift's Life and Works

1660	Restoration of Charles II and the Anglican Established Church. Foundation of Royal Society to promote investigation of science.
1662	Act of Uniformity bans nonconformists, making the Church of England more Royalist.
1663–1665	Clarendon Code of legalized measures biased against dissent. Religious assembly for worship or teaching was made virtually impossible.
1664	Swift's English parents, Jonathan and Abigail Erick, living in Dublin, marry.
1667	Father dies. Jonathan Swift born in Dublin. John Arbuthnot born.
1673–1682	Swift attends Kilkenny Grammar School. Late seventeenth-century classmates are William Congreve, George Berkeley, and George Farquhar.
1674	John Milton dies.
1677	John Bunyan's *Pilgrim's Progress*.
1678–1681	The Popish Plot conspiracy. Almost mass hysteria occurred in the belief in an imminent imposition of Catholic monarchy and suppression of Protestantism. Emergence of Whigs and Tories.
1682	Swift enters Trinity College, Dublin.
1685	Accession of James II. John Gay born.
1686	Swift graduates, Bachelor of Arts.
1688	Alexander Pope born. William Prince of Orange welcomed to England, James II flees. Civil war.
1689	William III accedes to throne. Swift becomes secretary to Sir William Temple at Moor Park.

1690	William defeats James at the Battle of the Boyne. Swift returns to Ireland seeking preferment. First onset of Ménières disease.
1691	Returns to Temple's patronage. Early *Odes* begun.
1692	Swift graduates Oxford, Master of Arts degree, the customary requirement for ordination. Jacobites defeated in Ireland.
1695	Ordained priest in Dublin. Takes up duties as prebend of Kilroot, near Belfast.
1696–1699	Returns to Moor Park. Writes *A Tale of a Tub. The Battle of the Books* written in support of Temple in the Ancients versus Moderns controversy, defending the superiority of ancient literature and learning against the claims of contemporary writers. The larger cultural significance of this divide is found throughout Swift's most important satire.
1697	William Dampier, *A New Voyage round the World.*
1699	Death of Temple. Swift returns to Dublin as chaplain to the Earl of Berkeley.
1700	Appointed vicar of Laracor and prebend of St. Patrick's, Dublin. John Dryden dies.
1701	*Contests and Dissensions . . . in Athens and Rome* published in England, defending impeached Whig leaders.
1702	Accession of Queen Anne. War of the Spanish Succession. Swift graduates Trinity, Doctor of Divinity.
1704	*A Tale of a Tub, The Battle of the Books,* and *The Mechanical Operation of the Spirit* published anonymously.
1707–1709	Ecclesiastical affairs in England. Swift gains a remission of church tax on the Irish clergy. Meets Joseph Addison, Richard Steele, and others. Swift writes *Bickerstaff Papers,* pamphlets on church and state.
1710	Robert Harley and Henry St. John, Lord Bolingbroke, form new Tory ministry. Swift's *Examiner* papers supporting Tories published. *Journal to Stella* begun.
1711	*Miscellanies in Prose and Verse. The Conduct of the Allies. An Argument against Abolishing Christianity.* Addison publishes the *Spectator.* Friendship with the leading political figures Harley and Bolingbroke.
1712	Meets Arbuthnot.
1713	Dean of St. Patrick's, Dublin. Swift, Pope, Gay, Arbuthnot, Harley, and Thomas Parnell form the "Martinus Scriblerus" Club, the meetings of which lead to satire on false learning that directly influences *Gulliver's Travels.*

Chronology

LITERARY AND HISTORICAL CONTEXT

1

Travelers, Geographers, Wonder, and Satire: The Background of *Gulliver's Travels*

Swift's most famous work confronts the reader with a basic question: Should it be assessed as a novel or a satire? Opting for one or the other entails applying conventionally appropriate criteria. The rise of the novel occurred in the eighteenth century, establishing standards of social realism and psychological consistency. If considered strictly in these terms, *Gulliver's Travels* seems to have many shortcomings. If, on the other hand, we view the story as a particular and general exposé of the vices and follies of rulers and politicians, individuals and societies, it seems to disallow the kind of literature Swift chose for his purposes.

We do not have to opt for or against the idea of a novel or satire. Moreover, we need not limit considerations of genre. There are different kinds of novel and different kinds of satire, from picaresque to romance, from formal verse satire to fantasy. If we widen the terms of investigation, it can be shown that *Gulliver's Travels* is a carefully calculated synthesis of many kinds of literature, including genuine accounts of travel, imaginative combinations of realism and fantasy, outright fantastic voyages, and utopian and anti-utopian ("dystopian") fables, which can idealize or satirize society or, indeed, do both.

The essential but difficult fact to grasp is that in what is now commonly known as the early modern period (1500–1750) preceding *Gulliver's Travels* (first published in 1726), there was no absolute distinction between the fantastic and the real. The mythical unicorn survived as the heavily real rhinoceros. The chameleon did not actually live on air, as Hamlet recalls, but it certainly changed its color. To some, *Gulliver's Travels* was immediately perceived as a satirical fantasy; yet to others it seemed very real. As Swift's friend, scientist and fellow satirist John Arbuthnot, wrote in a letter of 5 November 1726: "*Gulliver* is in everybody's hands. Lord Scarborough, who is no inventor of stories, told me that he fell in company with a master of a ship, who told him that he was very well acquainted with *Gulliver,* but that the printer had mistaken, that he lived in Wapping and not in Rotherhith. I lent the book to an old gentleman, who went immediately to his map to search for Lilliput."[1]

As heirs of a scientific and technological culture, today we accept only the verifiable facts of material reality. Thus the early astronauts brought back rocks from the surface of the moon. But what if such verification were unobtainable? Then authority answered the case— that is, the authority of written tradition: books.

TRAVELERS, GEOGRAPHERS, AND THE WONDROUS

At the close of *Gulliver's Travels* we hear from Gulliver, the putative author, that "I could perhaps, like others, have astonished thee with strange improbable tales," for, he continues, "It is easy for us who travel into remote Countries, which are seldom visited by *Englishmen* or other *Europeans,* to form Descriptions of wonderful Animals both at Sea and Land" (IV.xii.299). Gulliver insists that he is telling the truth. The allusions made here direct us to a vast body of travel literature that drew in part on a long-established tradition of geography and natural history. It is difficult to adequately categorize literature of this kind since there are so many overlapping boundaries. There are accounts of actual voyages by those who undertook them; reports of stories told to (but not experienced by) genuine voyagers; fictional stories drawing on first-hand reports of voyages believed to be real, but a medley of fact and fantasy; apparently true stories based on actual voyages, but with the deliberately added sensationalism of the fantastic; tales of imaginary voyages, grounding utopian fictions in materials from actual voyages; and so on.[2]

For example, take the strange case of Daniel Defoe's *Madagascar: or Robert Drury's Journal, during fifteen years captivity on that Island* (1729). As Defoe took the story of Alexander Selkirk's experience as a source for *Robinson Crusoe* (1719), so he expanded on a newspaper report of an abandoned ship's boy, adding adventures and local realism from other voyages, to produce *Madagascar*. *Madagascar* was accepted as authentic until the late nineteenth century. Eighteenth-century travelers vouched for its accuracy. It was read more than any other description of Madagascar and was used as a sourcebook by others. In adding to his original source, Defoe obtained information from sailors, concerning the language and customs of Madagascar, including details not found elsewhere. Though twentieth-century scholars have reassessed it as a fiction, it is considered to be the most "realistic" account of the country ever put together. Today in the cinema and on television we see the style of "documentary realism" that presents fiction as fact, but the eighteenth century, particularly in a man who called himself George Psalmanazar, took this concept further.

In Swift's satirical pamphlet *A Modest Proposal* the economist—who in Swift's time was referred to as projector—refers to the authority of "their famous Sallmanaazer, a Native of the Island Formosa." This "Formosan," Psalmanazar, whose real identity has eluded posterity, published *An Historical and Geographical Description of Formosa* in 1704. In the preface the author repudiates the "Romantic Stories" and "Fabulous Reports" of the East and gives a detailed account of Formosa—its language, customs, society, agriculture, and religion, including details of eating habits and child sacrifice. Psalmanazar became a London celebrity and, as a convert to Christianity, was sent to Oxford to teach Formosan—which was suspiciously like Greek—to missionaries. Embarrassingly, the whole thing was an imposture. Whoever Psalmanazar was, supposedly a Frenchman, he had made everything up, including the language. He had chosen Formosa as the place on which he would be an authority because it was hardly known to Europeans. Stricken with remorse, he confessed all in his *Memoirs*, published posthumously in 1765, though guilt had driven Psalmanazar to a penitential way of life earlier, in which he became a contrite dining companion of the sternly truthful Dr. Samuel Johnson.

The fabrications of Defoe, Psalmanazar, and others strove to reproduce the realism of actual contemporary voyage literature, which was based largely on empirical observation and the testimony of indigenous peoples. Reading was conditioned by the balance between credulity and scepticism. Credulity was influenced to some degree by the fact that all travelers had inherited a number of beliefs transmitted from antiquity through the Middle Ages. A brief sketch of this tradition provides a background for the credible and incredible in *Gulliver's Travels*.

In section III of *A Tale of a Tub* (1704), Swift's satire on abuses in learning and religion, a persona adopts the pedantic scholarly manner of a Dr. Bentley. In a re-reading of commentators of antiquity, Dr. Bentley refers to one Ctesias. Ctesias (fourth century B.C.) wrote a treatise on India that included all the folklore, tale, and legend up to his time concerning the marvels and wonders of the East.[3] This mythology permeated western Europe until discredited by empirical science. Here were found the fantastic creatures who were to haunt the European imagination for more than two thousand years: pygmies who fought with cranes (as Homer records in the *Iliad*); "sciapodes" who raised their single foot over their head as a parasol in the midday sun; the "cynocephali," men with dogs' heads who barked; headless people with their faces in their chest (the "anthropophagi" recalled by Othello); people with elephantine ears covering their upper body; giants; men with tails; people with reversed feet. Then there are the wondrous animals—unicorns, griffins, and the mortikhora, which had the face of a man, the body of a lion, and the tail of a scorpion.

Mixed with facts, Ctesias's marvels were repeated by Megasthenes, an ambassador, who had visited India in the first century A.D.

The greatest of Greek geographers, Strabo, in his *Geography* (first century A.D.) laughed at such apparent absurdities, but this work was lost until the Renaissance. Ctesias's wonders descended from authority to authority, the chiefest of whom was Pliny, with his *Natural History* (first century A.D.), in Latin. This influential source of knowledge was used by the medieval encyclopedists right up to Bartholomew the Englishman in the thirteenth century. Pliny's work is now remembered only for its fantastic eccentricities, yet it was once the greatest repository of knowledge known to humankind; the natural history of heaven and earth, from stars to stones, with thousand upon thousand of examples. Philemon Holland's seventeenth-century translation into English consists of 1,438 pages, measuring thirteen by nine by four inches and weighing ten pounds. The wonders of Ctesias now appeared in all forms of literature—encyclopedias, natural histories, cosmographies, and geographies—and on maps.

Pliny mentions the griffin, or gryphon (Bk. VII, ch. 2; Bk. X, ch. 72), a creature that appears in Western and Eastern mythology. At one extreme it is mythological or heraldic, combining lion's body, wings, and beaked head (an allegory of Christ in Dante's *Purgatorio,* canto XXIX); at another it is naturalistically conceived as a gigantic, eagle-like bird (associated with the Roc, or Ruk, of Eastern legend, which carried off Sinbad the Sailor in the *Arabian Nights*). In *The Book of Ser Marco Polo,* the Venetian traveler discusses the two versions of the creature: "The people of those isles call the bird *Ruc.* . . . So I wot not if this be the real gryphon, or if there be another manner of bird as great. But this I can tell you for certain, that they are not half lion and half bird as our stories do relate; but enormous as they be they are fashioned just like an eagle."[4]

The griffin appears on the best known of the medieval world maps, the *Mappa Mundi,* in Hereford Cathedral. On the 1459 map of Fra Mauro, who was patronized by the king of Portugal, the story of the bird big enough to carry off an elephant is inset by the southerly point of Africa. Theodor De Bry's 1594 map, included in his monumental *Great Voyages* (1590–1634), depicts Magellan on the deck of his ship, passing through what was then known as the Austral Sea, while a giant eagle-like bird is seen carrying off an elephant. In the superimposition of the real and the mythological, the fantastic is naturalized. Swift exploits this process in Gulliver's final misadventure in the second voyage, to Brobdingnag, the land of the giants. The caravan-like traveling room in which Gulliver is resting is carried off by a bird of Brobdingnagian proportions. Here Swift reproduces a tradition and echoes a major influence, Cyrano de Bergerac's *Histoire comique des états et empires de la lune* (1656; *Comic History of the Estates and Empires of the Moon*), in which the caged hero is carried off by the fabulous Roc. Swift narrows the gap between the credible and incredible by having Gulliver recount the events in naturalistic terms.

Marco Polo's account is one of the greatest travel books written, yet in the midst of his observations of the flora and fauna of Cathay and his record of the customs and habits of the Mongols are interspersed the old fables—in the kingdom of the Lambri are unicorns and men with tails, while on the island of Angamanain are to be found the cynocephali, barking men with dogs' heads. Marco Polo had one principle successor who was more responsible than anyone for ensuring the survival into the later Middle Ages of Ctesias's wonders. This was "Sir John Mandeville," an adopted name of the supposed author of the notorious *Travels* (thought to have been written in the fourteenth century). The influence of the *Travels* was incalculable. More than three hundred manuscripts of the account from before the age of printing survive; the advent of printing gave the work even more widespread and lasting popularity.

Mandeville took what he wanted from Marco Polo and added material from the journal of Friar Odoric, a missionary in Africa. To these were mixed in the fabulous beasts and men—giants, pygmies, griffins, dogs' heads, and the like. The only difference is that whereas Marco Polo and Friar Odoric were actual travelers, "Sir John Mandeville" never traveled anywhere. Yet his *Travels* was included in the first edition of one of the greatest collections of voyages put together in the Tudor period, that of Richard Hakluyt. Fantasy and fact were accorded the same status.

Trends in medieval geography paralleled those in the travel literature, since it was such books that were consulted as sources by those making maps. The renaissance in cartography that occurred in the fifteenth century was due in part to the rediscovery of Ptolemy's *Geography,* which had been lost to the West, though not to Arab civilization, since the second century A.D. Ptolemy's use of projection, the representation of a curved surface on a flat plane, in the depiction of the then known world, the Mediterranean coast bounded by the Pillars of Hercules, was forgotten. Diagrammatic Roman maps then gave rise to T/O maps, which derive from M. Vipsanius Agrippa (first century B.C.), son-in-law of the Emperor Augustus, whose *Orbis Terrarum,* or "survey of the world," was placed on public view in Rome and used by Pliny in his *Natural History.* The *T* placed in the O makes ⊕. The ⊕ represents the boundary of the known world; above the horizontal bar of the *T,* which represents a meridian from the river Don to the Nile, is the East; the vertical stroke represents the axis of the Mediterranean. Conforming to Christianity, Jerusalem is placed at the center, with Europe on one side, Africa on the other. To Latin Christendom the west was bounded by a mysterious ocean, the north by darkness, the east by Mongol hordes, and the south by infidel Muslims. The best-known T/O map produced by this culture was the *Mappa Mundi* of Hereford, on which are the wonders of Ctesias, removed from the east and spread around the farther reaches of the known world—soon to be transformed by the Age of Reconnaissance, the title coined by J. H. Parry for his authoritative study of the Renaissance geographical discoveries.[5]

Travelers and the Literature of Discovery

Voyagers in the later Middle Ages developed portolan maps, or charts, which were part of a navigator's manual of instructions.[6] Portolan charts used the newly developed compass readings of coastal bearings. These were limited by the absence of parallels and meridians, since the sphericity of the earth was ignored. Knowledge and use of latitudes was essential for ocean-going voyages of discovery, a need met eventually by Gerardus Mercator's projection. Preceding this were the four-

teenth-century Catalan world maps, named after the cartographers off
the Catalan coast based on the island of Majorca, which attempted to
incorporate knowledge of Asia derived from Marco Polo. The maps
were still influenced by predecessors; Jerusalem was the approximate
center of this world, but though the tribal lands of Gog and Magog are
there, the wonders of Ctesias are gone. Discoveries over three hundred
years, from approximately 1480 to 1780, from Diaz and Vasco da
Gama to Captain Cook, furnished data that largely mapped the modern world.

In the great discoveries of the Renaissance, taking the eastern
route round the Cape of Good Hope, Vasco da Gama reached India in
1497–99; the Portuguese reached China in 1514; and Cabral, on his
way to India, was blown by prevailing winds to within sight of Brazil
in 1500. Voyaging westward, Columbus discovered the Bahamas,
Cuba, Trinidad, and the "terrestrial paradise" of Venezuela (1492–98).
Magellan rounded Cape Horn, and the Pacific was opened to the
Western World. With the Spanish and Portuguese domination ratified
by the Papacy, northern explorers seeking a northwest passage discovered the "New World" of North America. With the new information
fed back to cartographers of Europe, there remained the problem of
representing the spiral curves of global measurement on the flat plane
of a map. Mercator's projection resolved this with his world map of
1569. (By increasing the distance between parallels proportionate to
the increase in the intervals between meridians from the equator to the
poles, the correct relationship of angles is preserved. Compared to
Mercator's world map, the Hereford *Mappa Mundi* is an unrecogniz-
able phantasmagoria.)

Mercator inherited a Greek idea—that there was an Australian
continent. How could the Greeks know this? The Hellenic view of
nature was symmetrical, and the Greeks believed that there must be a
habitable land mass in the Southern Hemisphere corresponding to that
in the north. Gulliver claims it as his personal belief that "it was ever my
Opinion, that there must be a Balance of Earth to counterpoise the great
Continent of *Tartary*" (II.iv.103). Though not then identified as a continent, Australia, Tasmania, and New Zealand were considered sizeable
enough, though by Swift's time only western Australia had been discov-

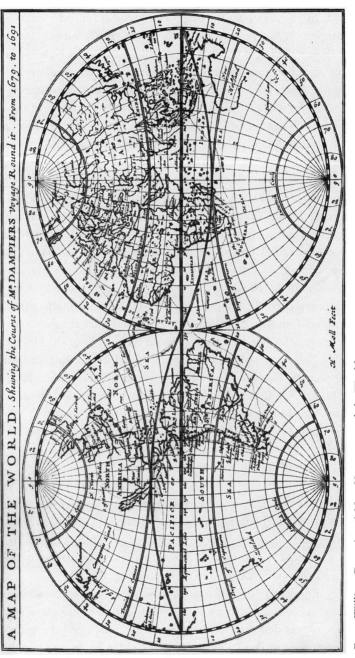

From William Dampier, *A New Voyage round the World.*

ered. In Hermann Moll's map of the world, reproduced in William Dampier's *A New Voyage round the World* (1697; see map, p. 11), as in *Gulliver's Travels,* it is called New Holland. Australia/New Holland had a great importance for utopian writing, including *Gulliver's Travels;* because it was unknown, it could be peopled by the imagination.

In the wake of the discoveries followed publication of the various voyages. Foremost of the English collections was Richard Hakluyt's *The Principall Navigations, Voyages, Traffiques and Discoveries of the English Nation* (1589), followed by folios of 1598 and 1600. Here was a patriotic celebration of the derring-do by land and sea of the English (and Welsh) since the early centuries, not just the great names of Raleigh, Drake, Hawkins, Frobisher, and the Cabots. Tucked away in the three thousand pages of a modern edition is a letter to Hakluyt from Gerardus Mercator advising on the possibility of a northeast passage, citing the authority of Pliny, no less.

In *Some thoughts concerning reading and discovery for a Gentleman* (1693), the philosopher John Locke remarks that "To the reading of history, chronology and geography are absolutely necessary. In geography, we have two general ones in English, Heyl[y]n and Moll." Hermann Moll, a Dutchman domiciled in England, supplied the map for Dampier's volume. He was the leading British mapmaker of his day. Gulliver somewhat arrogantly relates geographical information "communicated many Years ago to my worthy Friend Mr. *Hermann Moll* . . . although he hath rather chosen to follow other Authors" (IV.xi.292). Peter Heylyn's *Cosmographie* of 1652 was an enlargement of an earlier *Geography.* His lengthy introduction includes the fruits of Renaissance discovery and rediscovery. Strabo is praised as well as Pliny, and for cartography Heylyn turns to Mercator and his fellow Fleming, Abraham Ortelius. In the chapter on India, Heylyn dismisses the "monstrous Fables" of Ctesias, listing his fantastic creatures as "impossible and incredible" impostures of so-called geographers who lacked any real knowledge.

Knowledge of the world was pursued by voyagers sponsored by the Royal Society of London, whom Gulliver emulates. The Royal Society was dedicated to experimental science and the gathering of empirical data. This knowledge was sought in books, not least by Swift, who owned a number of volumes devoted to seventeenth-century voyages. It was not until 1979, however, that any Swift scholar undertook a systematic scrutiny of these volumes, which was painstakingly carried out by Arthur Sherbo, to whom part of the following information is indebted.[7] Swift also owned the massive collections of Hakluyt and those of his successor, Samuel Purchas, who literally inherited some of Hakluyt's documents, subsequently publishing an equally voluminous collection of voyages, *Hakluytus Posthumous, or Purchas his Pilgrims* (1625), details of which influenced *Gulliver's Travels.*

Gulliver's Travels takes great pains to copy mostly seventeenth-century predecessors to establish a concrete geographical setting against which Swift can place fantastic materials for the ulterior purpose of satire. Unfortunately, an inconsistency at the beginning of the book has confused responses to Swift's method. The four engravings of the maps made on behalf of Benjamin Motte, who first published *Gulliver's Travels* in 1726, are inconsistent with the details of the text. Did Swift deliberately plan such error as part of the satire, or, as Arthur E. Case argues, did Swift intend that the maps should be part of the realistic setting for the satire?[8] Although Swift apparently made no attempt to correct the maps for the edition published by George Faulkner in 1735, Case believes that Swift had no part in these illustrations of 1726 and that he consistently worked out where he wished the various lands to be placed in relation to Moll's map. Houyhnhnmland is seen to be due west of Tasmania. Placing the rationalist horses in this part of the then unknown world presents a challenge to seventeenth-century utopian texts similarly placed.

Swift refers to "my cousin Dampier," and scholars have made stylistic comparisons with parts of *A New Voyage round the World.* The parodic and competitive relationship between Defoe's *Robinson Crusoe* (1719) and Swift's work, and Swift's reference to Dampier, is intended to encourage this comparison since there was a well-known connection between Defoe's work and the famous mariner-explorer-buccaneer. Alexander Selkirk, the prototype for Crusoe, was sailing master on a privateering expedition round Cape Horn of 1703; Dampier was commander of the two vessels, which eventually parted company. After a violent row on his ship, Selkirk was abandoned on the island of Juan Fernandez. After four years as castaway he was picked up in 1709 by another privateer, with Dampier on board as pilot. Captain Woodes Rogers's account of the rescue inspired Defoe. Gulliver's "I have not been so studious of Ornament as of Truth" (IV.xii.299) agrees with Dampier's "a Plain and Just Account of the true Nature and State of the Things described, than of a Polite and Rhetorical Narrative." Again, Gulliver's disingenuous assertion that his "Story could contain little besides common Events, without those ornamental Descriptions of strange Plants, Trees, Birds and other Animals; or the barbarous Customs and Idolatry of Savage People, with which most Writers abound" (II.viii.143) compares with Dampier's preface to *A Voyage to New-Holland* (1699), where he states that his account "may in some measure be acceptable to Candid and Impartial Readers, who are curious to know the Nature of the Inhabitants, Animals, Plants, Soil etc. in those distant countries."

Arthur Sherbo shows that Dampier was writing according to the conventions established by contemporaries and predecessors, although he was not the stereotypical mariner. Dampier was effectively a pirate for several years, yet he was a man of some learning, as were many who joined in these expeditions. These seamen-narrators nearly always adopted a mode of address to the "curious" and "candid" reader, following dedicatory and prefatorial material in which the common stance was that of probity and experience condemning fabulous romances. Common to most was jingoistic patriotism, though material self-interest often provided the impetus for adventure. In comparison, Gulliver's expression as narrator is conventional, particularly in the accurate description of land and sea. Therefore, rather than seeing *Gulliver's Travels* as a parody of a specific work, it is more appropriate to recognize Swift's synthesis of various voyagers' words and matter.

In Purchas there are several accounts of pygmies and giants, but none in Dampier. Turning to Swift's choice of names for the ships in *Gulliver's Travels*, the *Antelope* appears in Dampier, the *Hope-well*, the *Adventure*, and the *Swallow* in Purchas and Hakluyt. Two men by the name of Mendez appear in Purchas. In an interpretation of Gulliver's fourth voyage, Don Pedro de Mendez, the humane, gentle, and long-suffering Portuguese captain, is crucial. In a few instances

Swift's borrowing from travel literature is extensive and unquestionable. For example, it is long established that the account of the storm at the opening of the voyage to Brobdingnag, with its seemingly excessive and parodic use of nautical detail, is taken almost verbatim from Samuel Sturmy's *Mariner's Magazine* of 1669. There are other parodies in *Gulliver's Travels*, which will be discussed shortly; the following instances indicate the problem of source attribution.

At the beginning of the voyage to the Houyhnhnms, Gulliver relates how the monkey-like Yahoos "leaped up into the Tree, from whence they began to discharge their Excrements on my Head" (IV.i.226). Critics and editors have noted Swift's ownership of Lionel Wafer's *New Voyage and Description of the Isthmus of America* (1699). Like Gulliver, Wafer became both a surgeon and a captain, and in his account he describes monkeys "pissing down purposely on our heads." Wafer thus appears to be a direct source, but Dampier also describes Panamanian monkeys, "dancing from Tree to Tree, over my Head; chattering and making a terrible Noise . . . others scattered their Urine and Dung about my Ears." Swift seems to have combined these accounts with those he had read of the ugly and bestial Hottentots in South Africa to create the Yahoo.

Gulliver records of the Yahoo females that "Their dugs [breasts] hung between their fore feet, and often reached almost to the ground as they walked" (IV.i.225), a description close to that of the many reports of the Hottentots. Yet we find a comparable source in Richard Ligori's widely read account of slave workers in *A True and Exact History of the Island of Barbados* (1657): "their breasts hung down below their Navels, so that when they stoop at their common work of weeding, they hang almost to the ground."

Again, in the *Collection of Voyages and Travels*, produced by the brothers Awnsham and John Churchill in 1704, is found Dr. Francis Careri's *Voyage round the World*, in which the author relates that the Dutch, to exclude fellow Christian traders, urged the Japanese "to lay a Crucifix on the Ground at the Landing Place, to discover whether any Christian comes under a disguise, because any such will refuse, or at least make a difficulty to trample on the Crucifix to enter *Nangasache*, the Port of Japan." Gulliver had asked to be excused from the practice of *"trampling upon the Crucifix"* (III.xi.217) in his application for safe conduct to Nangasac. In Engelbert Kaempfer's *History of Japan* (1727), however, which some believe Swift knew in manuscript, the author describes the same practice, though Swift's echoing of a graphic verb—"trampling"—seems to indicate the former as source.

All of the above notwithstanding, Swift, in "A Letter from Capt. Gulliver to His Cousin Sympson," which he added to the Faulkner 1735 edition of *Gulliver's Travels*, signaled in several ways something other than a straightforward account of voyaging. Not least because William Sympson was the spurious author of *A New Voyage to the East-Indies* (1715), a plagiarism of another work. For those who could not identify this imposture, Faulkner added a notorious portrait, that of Capt. Lemuel Gulliver, beneath which appeared the legend *"Splendide Mendax,"* or "Magnificient Liar."

TRAVELERS AND SATIRE,
UTOPIA AND THE NATURE OF MAN

Travel, satire, and utopia have always been interrelated. As mythology and travel coincided in something like Homer's *Odyssey,* so various wondrous places filled the reader's imagination—the Fortunate Isles, the Isles of the Blessed, Thule, Ogygia. The biblical paradise provided another idealized location that was happily accommodated by the pastoral description of the "pleasaunce," the *locus amoenus* ("pleasant place") of classical rhetoric. Virgil's Elysian Fields were adapted by Christian poets to this pagan conception of paradise. With the Renaissance discoveries, Eden was eventually removed from its biblical location and eagerly sought as far afield as Columbus's Venezuela and, in due course, Tahiti.

As a counterpart to perfection in nature men sought perfection in society; sometimes the two could be portrayed together in something as powerful and haunting as the notion of the Golden Age—as recorded by Ovid, for example, in the *Metamorphoses*—man, beast, and nature in peace, perfection, and harmony. Such utopian dreams were more practically confronted in another great source of Western speculation, Plato's *Republic,* and were actually claimed as historically real-ized in Plutarch's representation of a Spartan utopia in his *Life of Lycurgus.* Much of *Gulliver's Travels* incorporates satire on utopian lit-erature, the voyage to the Houyhnhnms particularly having a close relation to the traditions of satire and utopian writing from Plato and Plutarch to seventeenth-century Deist utopias.

One problem in considering satire is that the word *satirical* often seems more suitable. Strictly speaking, *satire* is not a genre in the clear-ly defined sense in which we may talk about the sonnet, for example. There are, of course, satiric traditions. In his *Discourse Concerning the Original and Progress of Satire* (1693), still one of the best introduc-tions to the subject, John Dryden devotes most of his attention to the formal verse satire of the Roman poets Horace and Juvenal. In recent decades, however, there has been a growing recognition of the satire associated with Lucian, whose work was a great influence on Swift and others. The satirical response to idealized literature began most forcibly in antiquity with him.

Three classical writers, Menippus (Greek, third century B.C.), Varro (Roman, first century B.C.), and Lucian (Greek, second century A.D.), have given their names to forms of satire known as Menippean, Varronian, and Lucianic. Varro, however, called his writing "Menippean satire" (*sat-urae menippeae*), of which only fragments remain. Lucian's work is regarded as the most significant corpus of Menippean satire, since next to nothing by Menippus himself survives. The term *Menippean* has come to absorb the word *Lucianic* partly as a result of Mikhail Bakhtin's usage in his *Problems of Dostoevsky's Poetics* (1984), which has been very influen-tial in the modern development of the theory of fiction.

Since it is characterized by heterogeneity, Menippean satire does not easily lend itself to definition. Within that heterogeneity, however, are found such modes as the fantastic voyage, dialogues of the dead, dream visions, and mock utopias. In prose and verse, the Menippean satire was comic and satirical, yet ultimately serious in the constant challenge it presented by debunking philosophy and ideas. In range it could move from low-life naturalism reminiscent of the picaresque novel to topicality to a detached, otherworldly view of human little-ness in life and art. Parody and paradox were favorite weapons of the

Menippean satirist. From the Renaissance to the eighteenth century the names most frequently associated with the mode are Erasmus, Rabelais, Swift himself, Voltaire, and Laurence Sterne.

Though Menippus himself appears in several of Lucian's dialogues and in his lunar fantasy *Icaromenippus,* Lucian's *True History* has been most influential, particularly in the seventeenth century and in Swift. The *True History* offers a parodic rebuttal to what Lucian skeptically sees as the tall stories of figures like Herodotus the historian and Ctesias. For Lucian, "their guide and instructor in this sort of charlatanry is Homer's Odysseus." The travelers in the fantastic voyages of the *True History* arrive at a strange Ovidian island in the western ocean and then, by way of a whirlwind, fly on a voyage to the moon. This became a convention of the genre, for example, in Cyrano and Bishop Godwin. A war between the rulers of the moon and the sun is carried out by various fantastic creatures: grassplume birds with wings like lettuce leaves, flea-archers mounted on fleas as big as twelve elephants, millet shooters and garlic fighters, a flying infantry borne aloft by inflatable tunics, and so on. The moon is entirely male, since children are born from the calf of the male leg. In further adventures the voyagers are marooned inside the belly of a 150-mile-long whale, complete with warring societies, rivers, islands, and forests. Elsewhere, in Lamptown, there are no recognizable people, only speaking lamps. Parodying the report of a flying island in Herodotus, Lucian has huge giants row a complete island as if it were a boat, with full-grown cypress trees as oars. They unsuspectingly moor the island to a whale, another convention, popularized by the widespread story of the voyage of St. Brendan, which also appears in Milton's portrayal of Leviathan in *Paradise Lost* (Bk. I, ll. 200–208). (In the tenth-century tale of his fantastic voyage, St. Brendan encounters the whale while searching for the beautiful Land of Promise in the Atlantic.) In an important sequence, while on the Island of the Blessed, the heroes, poets, and philosophers of antiquity are questioned by the travelers.

William A. Eddy argues that an important additional influence on Swift was the sequel to the *True History,* added by Nicolas Perrot d'Ablancourt (c. 1648) in translating and publishing an edition in French (1707), which Swift bought in 1711.[9] Swift, like Lucian, is partly parodying a form of literature. Gulliver caught up in the wars between Lilliput and Blefuscu is reminiscent of the traveler's position in the war between the sun and the moon. Flying and floating islands in each seem related, while the vision of the heroes on Glubbdubdrib strongly echoes that of Lucian's traveler's experience on the Island of the Blessed. D'Ablancourt's sequel provides further detail that Swift took up, namely, voyages to an island of animals and adjacent islands of giants, magicians, and pygmies. There are both likenesses and differences in d'Ablancourt and Swift. Without insisting on d'Ablancourt's sequel as a sole source, it appears self-evident that his fourfold division therein of societies of pygmies, giants, magicians, and animals provided a creative impetus for Swift, contributing to the synthesis of *Gulliver's Travels* as a whole.

In the tradition of extraordinary voyages, perhaps most important of all for Swift were the two posthumously published works of Cyrano de Bergerac, *Histoire comique des états et empires de la lune* (cited earlier) and *Histoire comique des états et empires du soleil* (1657; *Comic History of the Estates and Empires of the Sun*). Cyrano was inspired by the Menippean satire of an Englishman, Bishop Francis Godwin, whose *The Man in the Moon* (1638) provided an immediate prototype. The society of moon dwellers presents a crimeless idyll with a natural abundance of food, minimal work, beautiful females, and eternal spring—a utopian element of increasing importance in such seventeenth-century portrayals. As there is no crime, there are no lawyers; physicians are unnecessary since the Lunarians live healthily according to nature. Upon death—and this is quite close to Swift's Houyhnhnms—there is no grief but a kind of rejoicing at passing into heaven. Compared with this utopianism, which will be developed shortly in relation to realistic voyages, Cyrano is strongly satirical. Passing consideration of Defoe's *The Consolidator* (1705) may be made for the contrast with Bishop Godwin, for here the society found on the moon is far from utopian. It is an allegory of English society, complete with Deists and High and Low Churchmen, a mode Swift was to explore with the terrestrial analogue of Lilliput, particularly.

Swift took from Cyrano the situation found in the *Histoire comique de la lune* for much of the circumstances of the voyage to Brobdingnag. Cyrano travels to the moon and discovers giants, one of whom immediately exhibits him for money. He meets a dwarf who is identified as Bishop Godwin's traveler, Gonzales. He is taken to court and becomes the queen's pet. A young giantess falls in love with him. These and other details are so close to those characterizing Swift's second voyage that even though Swift never mentions Cyrano, or owned a copy of his story, attribution of source is unavoidable. Cyrano's second work, the *Histoire comique des états et empires du soleil*, is in part directly comparable with Gulliver's experience in Houyhnhnmland. In the land of the birds on the sun, Cyrano is put on trial for the vices of humanity. Though defended by one bird, Cyrano tries to evade censure by pretending that he is not a debased man but an innocent monkey. Gulliver as a seeming Yahoo is permanently on trial before Houyhnhnmland reason and eventually finds himself condemned along with all Yahoo kind. Within the genre of the fantastic voyage, though strange creatures are encountered, beast kingdoms are rare. Swift took the precedent of Cyrano one step further by portraying homo sapiens as the degraded filthy Yahoo, with which Gulliver finally identifies. In addition, Swift presents in the Houyhnhnms both a critique of humankind and a utopian ideal for Gulliver. Swift directs his satire at utopianism in general and the utopian voyage in particular.

Sir Thomas More's best-known work, *Utopia* (1516), gave the English language a new word. More carefully chose a Greek word by which he could pun on the ideas of "no place" (*ou-topos*) and "good place" (*eu-topos*). Such humanist wit exploits the double-edged possibility of portraying a seeming ideal while actually satirizing travelers' tales and English society. Raphael Hythloday, More's traveler, is a Portuguese mariner who claims to have been a member of Amerigo Vespucci's voyage to America, at which he leaves the main expedition and travels on to the land of King Utopas. Given that the "hero's" surname means "skilled in nonsense," however, the educated reader would have been cautious about accepting everything he says at face value. Swift deeply admired the moral and spiritual integrity of More in the face of political tyranny under Henry VIII, and on Glubbdubdrib, in a passage indebted to Lucian, Gulliver learns from Brutus that he, Socrates, More, and others "were perpetually together: A *Sextumvirate* to which all the Ages of the World cannot add a Seventh" (III.vii.196).

The Background of Gulliver's Travels

In book 2 of *Utopia* Hythloday presents a society enlightened by a communistic sense of public good, looking back to Stoicism and forward to Marxism. As such it is in contrast with the rampant materialism and power hunger of fifteenth-century Europe, exemplified particularly in the rapacious enclosures in England furthering lucrative pasture for wool at the expense of yeoman tillage. The Utopians hold wealth in contempt—gold jewelry is viewed as a bauble for children. Unlike feudal Europe, Utopia is a democracy supervised by philosopher-guardians, recalling Plato's *Republic.* More's *Utopia* is thought out in largely secular, humanist lines. Whereas some later utopias explore specifically Christian ideals, like Johann Valentin Andreae's *Christianopolis* (1619) and Tommaso Campanella's *The City of the Sun* (1602–27), a progressive scientific element that is found in Andreae is developed in Francis Bacon's *New Atlantis* (1627). More important for *Gulliver's Travels* was the appearance of fictions that combine realist voyage narrative with the discovery of utopian societies. The two most significant are Gabriel Foigny's *La Terre Australe connue* (1676) and Denis Vairasse d'Alais's *L'Histoire des Sévarambes* (1677), which had actually appeared in English two years earlier as *The History of the Sevarites, or Sevarambi.*

The utopias of Andreae and Campanella are Christian, of a mystical and universalistic kind, and within the secularized humanism of More's *Utopia* religious pluralism is encouraged. In Foigny and Vairasse is something markedly different—and anathema to Swift—an explicit commendation of Deism and an implicit condemnation of Christianity. Deism has been mentioned several times. It is worth going over its meaning to ensure the force of the following points. Coined from the Latin *deus,* or god, Deism is the belief in a god, or Supreme Being, without faith in revealed religion. By revealed religion is meant the revelation of the incarnation, ministry, and Passion of Christ, the Redemption Christ undertook for all humanity on his own death, and Resurrection. This is revealed in the words of the Gospels. To some degree Swift's presentation of the rationalist utopia of the Houyhnhnms is a dystopian counterblast to the Deist utopias of his French predecessors, a position Swift also indicates by placing his utopia in unexplored Australia.

Jacques Sadeur, Foigny's hero, relates his adventures and misadventures from his deathbed.[10] Initially, Foigny borrows from a contemporary Portuguese narrative of a real voyage to provide a convincing maritime background—much like Swift. We are plunged into the wonders of the Congo—springs of wine, colored sheep, and stripe-legged Kaffirs. More conventionally, there appears the whale as an island and then the Roc bird, which carries off the hero to Australia. Here Sadeur finds a spiritual home, since he, like the Australians, is hermaphroditic. These people live in nude equality and liberty, free from disease, on a fruit diet in a climate of perpetual spring. The hermaphrodites, modeled on Plato's Androgynes, in uniting both sexes, are free from all the strife between men and women. In contrast, Europeans have only half a sex each and are thus "half-men," like the beasts. Sadeur encounters a venerable old sage who espouses their religion of pacific Deism in contrast with all the war, rapine, crime, disorder, and unhappiness of Europeans. The inference is that revealed religion causes suffering. Eventually Sadeur, like Gulliver, is put on trial and found wanting. Geographical discoveries of the Renaissance had shown that there were people, like the Incas and the Tartars, whose faith in a god did not rely on revealed religion. Even more puzzlingly subversive were the Buddhists, those most holy of men who did not seem to have a god at all. For rationalist freethinkers like Foigny and Vairasse, such facts clearly undermined the absolute claims of Christianity.

Like Foigny, Vairasse recounts the posthumously published memoirs of one Captain Siden. Another identifiable contemporary source is used for realism, but Vairasse chooses not to indulge in the fantastic adventures of his predecessor, concentrating on social and geographic facts. In his sojourn among the Severambe people of Australia, the captain discovers a society regulated by a benevolent despot-supervisor, the Viceroy of the Sun, who distributes necessary goods equally among his people. These sun worshippers are innocent and tranquil, temperate and honest, enjoying a sex life regulated by law, since celibacy is the only evil. Though the sun is the Inca-like object of worship, Nature is the god of the Severambites, not nature as phenomena but nature as a rational principle of creation. If god is known but not by faith in revealed religion, then by what means? Reason was always the answer, but instead of being a conventional "handmaid" to faith, with Deism it came to displace faith, and Christ was made redundant. Vairasse's critique of European Christianity appears most forcefully in the account of the impostures of Omigas, the predecessor of Sevarias, who brought the wisdom of Deism. The "miracles" of Omigas offer a crudely powerful critique of biblical miracles and the miracle of Christ's incarnation. Omigas "pretended that he was the son of the Sun." In short, Omigas offered superstition, Sevarias brought enlightenment.

Gulliver's voyage to the Houyhnhnms is generally regarded as the most complex of the *Travels,* so much so that there are still polarized critical views on what the horses' republic actually amounts to. But on one issue there is some agreement. To a degree the satire of part IV is aimed at the notion of a rationalist utopia. How far this implies a satire on Deism is still debated. Swift was an orthodox Christian, a believer in revealed religion, committed to the ordinances of the Anglican Church. To him, and many of his contemporaries, Deism was not just a form of natural piety but disguised atheism, or "freethinking," as it was called in his day. Perhaps Swift deliberately chose to place his dystopia in Tasmania, then considered part of Australia, as a challenge to the Australian utopias of Foigny and Vairasse.

Houyhnhnm society is founded on reason. Its "grand Maxim is, to cultivate *Reason,* and to be wholly governed by it" (IV.vii.272–73). This rational principle is realized by friendship, benevolence, and temperance; industry, exercise, and cleanliness. In contrast, for all his seeming differences, Gulliver is adjudged to be a Yahoo, Swift's symbol for ultimate human bestiality, filth, and depravity. An analysis of the dystopian elements will be made later, but here it is important to point out the further cultural backgrounds Swift is drawing on—what is called "theriophily," which is related to beast fables and "the nature of man" question.

Theriophily, which means love of animals, is a word coined to denote that tradition in Western literature in which the beasts are seen to be superior to humankind. The tradition arose in large part in reaction to the Circe myth in Homer's *Odyssey.* Circe's transformation of some of Ulysses' men into pigs was commonly read as an allegorical revelation of the bestial nature of humankind. Some thought this a little unfair to pigs, and thus Plutarch in his *Gryllus* laid the foundation for the literature of theriophily in the pig's assertion of superiority, not defense of inferiority, over humans. In 1549 G. B. Gelli published his *Circe,* considerably adding to the work of his predecessor by having Ulysses interview a large number of animals, only one of whom wishes to return to humankind, the philosopher-elephant who values human reason. Perhaps most important of all is Montaigne's championing of such ideas in his essays "On Pedantry" and "On the Cannibals" and in his most influential work, *An Apology for Raimond de Sebonde* (1569).

In brief, theriophily finds various arguments for the superiority of animals: they are stronger, speedier, and happier; they do not have envy, pride, hatred, greed, and so on. Gulliver's Houyhnhnm master goes over in detail the physical shortcomings of this Yahoo manqué: the uselessness of his nails; the weakness of feet needing covers; the necessity of clothing, etc. But the Bible teaches that humankind has dominion over the beasts, and pagan philosophy insists that humankind is the only *rational* animal. To counter this, theriophilists argued that the beasts do have reason, citing instances like the fox listening on ice for the sound of running water and "reasoning" that if it is heard, the ice is too thin. Did not the faithful dog demonstrate an ability for syllogistic reasoning? The master having taken one of three divergent paths, the hound vainly sniffs two for scent and then bounds up the third without repeating the test. What is more, do not the beasts actually teach men? They build, they weave, and they know which herbs will heal wounds. Those in despair at the corruption of humanity believed they could find evidence for the opposite in the animal kingdom, as Gulliver does in his discovery of "the perfection of nature," the Houyhnhnm in his Spartan utopia. With this polarity Swift engaged with what is called "the nature of man" debate.

Is man good or is he irredeemably bad? If neither absolutely, then what kind of balance, or imbalance, is there between the two? This inescapable polarity is part of the Western conception of humankind. Classical antiquity propounded the humanist notion of man, at his best, as the dignified bearer of reason. Christianity was built on the Hebraic notion of the Fall, in which the inherited original sin of Eden ensured humanity's sinful corruption. In the early conciliar movements of the church, which were to establish doctrines for a thousand years, St. Augustine's view of human being's natural depravity defeated Pelagius, who denied the inheritance of original sin. Eventually, at the center of the Reformation, Luther debated with Erasmus on the nature of human will. For the German it was enslaved by sin, for the Dutch humanist it was free. English Calvinists took a harsh, predestinarian view and were opposed by Arminians like Milton, who, though a Puritan, insisted on freedom of the will.

In seventeenth-century England there developed a correlation to this in the debate concerning the so-called "decay of nature." Godfrey Goodman's *The Fall of Man* (1616) took the pessimistic view, supported by the doctrine of human depravity, that nature was in a state of increasing decay and corruption. George Hakewill's *An Apologie of the Power and Providence of God* (1627) opposed this belief, which is central to the "ancients'" point of view, with his "modern" idea of progress, albeit circular rather than linear (rise-fall-renewal-rise . . .). Puritan extremists took the hard line, which was in the latter half of the seventeenth century opposed by the appearance of a group of Anglican churchmen called Latitudinarians, from the wish, voiced by Archbishop Tillotson, that "latitude" should be shown in judging human weakness. For someone of Swift's conviction and temperament vice should be punished, not mollified. In the political and moral spheres we find Thomas Hobbes's doctrine of humankind's essential power hunger and natural egotism, which was opposed by the third Earl of Shaftesbury's philosophical endorsement of humankind as altruistic and benevolent in his *Characteristics* (1711). These positions debating the nature of humanity were fought out on various platforms for the first half of the eighteenth century, with Dr. Johnson fighting a rearguard action later on against the overpowering benevolence, sensibility, and progress that had triumphed. Swift's stern, uncompromising view, of both humankind and the satirist's obligation, is encapsulated in one of the most quoted sections of *Gulliver's Travels,* the King of Brobdingnag's summary reply to Gulliver's panegyric on the status quo of England in the 1720s: "I

cannot but conclude the Bulk of your Natives to be the most pernicious Race of little odious Vermin that Nature ever suffered to crawl
upon the Surface of the Earth" (II.vi.126).

Gulliver's interview with the King of Brobdingnag reverses an
actual situation of 1693, when Swift was delegated to explain to
William III, who had vetoed some parliamentary bills, the workings of
British government. After Gulliver's panegyric the King of Brobdingnag had systematically revealed the corrupt reality of British institutions. Before William the young Swift explained the nature of a
parliamentary bill designed to ensure that government remained free
from corruption. William was no philosopher king, but the political
philosophy of the Glorious Revolution had utopian elements in which
Swift was an ardent believer. From the perspective of the 1720s, for
Swift the reality had become dystopian corruption.

In *Gulliver's Travels* Swift alludes several times in a generalized
fashion to seventeenth-century European history. Then in his mid-
fifties, Swift had in his lifetime witnessed the most momentous period
for British and world history since the rejection of the Stuarts and the
foundation of constitutional monarchy began what was eventually to
evolve as a model of parliamentary democracy.

Swift was born into the post-1660 world of restored Stuart
monarchy and the reestablishment of Anglican episcopacy. The Puritan
republican experiment, which entailed the execution of Charles I, had
failed, leaving, for Swift, the legacy of the atrocity of fanaticism and
the constant threat to the established church in the social, political,
and religious divisiveness of nonconformity and dissent. Nonconformity was viewed by Anglicans not just as difference of opinion over
Christian worship and church organization but as the threat of bloody
revolution overturning all social structures that would lead to the barbaric anarchy of something like the German Anabaptists of sixteenth-
century Münster. On the other hand, the rumored association of the
Stuarts with Catholicism and the French court presented the dangers
of absolutism and popery. In his boyhood Swift would have absorbed
the hysteria of the Popish Plot of 1679—the belief that Catholics
would install a Catholic monarch, suppress Protestantism, and destroy
Parliament. The fact of an impending Catholic king in James, Duke of

York, Charles II's brother, led to the Exclusion Crisis of 1679 and the formation of the Whig and Tory parties, the former bent on ensuring the exclusion of any papal dynasty. As a young man in the Ireland of the 1680s, Swift would have readily acknowledged the threat of popery to church and state. James II did succeed to the throne, and the absolutist threat to liberty and property became apparent to all when the monarch claimed such "rights" as dispensing with the law.

The political philosophy of those usually called "Old Whigs," the political principles evolved by leading figures like the first Earl of Shaftesbury and John Locke in the Exclusion Crisis, now became the guiding power behind the invitation to William of Orange to save England from tyranny and slavery. The bloodless Glorious Revolution took place with the accession of William and Mary, and the Declaration of Rights was followed eventually at Queen Anne's accession by the Act of Settlement of 1701, which ensured the continuation of Protestant constitutional monarchy in the dynasty of the House of Hanover with the eventual succession of King George I on the death of Anne in 1714.

The Old Whigs believed in England as a mixed monarchy containing the balanced elements of king, lords, and commons. The monarch observed a contract between himself and the ruled, to observe the law and ensure protection of property and liberty of the subject. Tories believed in the divine right of kingship and consequently advocated doctrines of passive obedience and nonresistance. For the Old Whigs the king must not encroach on Parliament. Implicit in Tory adulation was the idea that the king's prerogatives were paramount. Swift subscribed to Old Whig revolutionary principles but only gradually came to realize that, even though befriended by them, he was out of step with the "Modern Whigs" of Queen Anne's reign. The Modern Whigs drew considerable political and financial support from nonconformists and dissenters—all in all the new monied men of commerce whom Swift believed thrived by continuing the warmongering policies supporting Marlborough and the War of the Spanish Succession. As a consequence, Swift was drawn to the Tory administration of Robert Harley in 1710, which he supported extensively in his series of *Examiner* papers.

Harley had led what was known as the "Country" opposition to William III, which supported such policies as the landed conservative objection to standing armies in time of peace (a policy queried by the King of Brobdingnag). Harley had also been in large part responsible for the details of the Act of Settlement. Initially supporting the Modern Whigs out of favor in Anne's coalition government, Swift's disillusionment was matched by that of Harley, who moved from an Old Whig position of the 1690s into the "Country" alliance of opposition Whigs and Tories whose basic ideology was an idealized patriotism that aspired to rise above the cut and thrust of day-to-day party politics. The Tories were victors in the elections of 1711, and Harley, after successfully dealing with Swift over Church of Ireland ecclesiastical business, persuaded him to champion the administration in his writings. In a sense this resolved the anomaly in Swift's own position, since, as a member of the established church, he had always been a self-professed Tory High Church Anglican, in opposition to the Low Church members, who favored the Whigs.

For a few years Swift enjoyed the patronage of the great, hobnobbing with the likes of Henry St. John, Viscount Bolingbroke, but a bishopric was not forthcoming—Queen Anne had hated the impiety of *A Tale of a Tub.* With the advent of George I and the Whigs in 1714, who remembered Swift's anti-war writings, the days of glory were over, and Swift returned to his "exile" in Dublin. For someone who believed that political ideals had indeed been realized in a Glorious Revolution and subsequently compromised by corrupt administrations, the spectacle of the Whigs and Hanoverians in the 1720s and the injustices of Ireland were grist for a satirical mill. As a bishop, Swift would probably have left volumes of dutiful though unread sermons, but as dean of St. Patrick's (from 1713) he left us one of the greatest and most-read satires in English literature. The church's loss was the world's gain.

2

The Importance of *Gulliver's Travels*

The importance of *Gulliver's Travels* derives from many factors. Arguably Swift's greatest satire, it is certainly the most read of his works. Satire characterized the "Augustan," or neoclassical, period of English literature from approximately 1660 to 1745, and *Gulliver* is usually placed alongside John Gay's *The Beggar's Opera* (1728) and Pope's *Dunciad* (1728), together comprising the consummate triumvirate of that mode. Again, literary historians looking at the development of prose fiction in this period acknowledge that John Bunyan's *The Pilgrim's Progress* (1678), Daniel Defoe's *Robinson Crusoe* (1719), and *Gulliver's Travels* were overwhelmingly popular at every level of readership, from children to the royal family. Indeed, all three have become children's classics, usually illustrated in abridged form.

The inventiveness of Swift's imagination, particularly in the first two voyages, has always delighted readers avid for the thrills of adventure—surprise, danger, and escape in extraordinary circumstances. Adults without any particularly close knowledge of the political or literary background are able to respond at various levels, beyond the adventure, as the continued publication of the work demonstrates: *Gulliver's Travels* is currently available in fifty adult and children's editions in the United Kingdom and the United States—an extraordinary figure for an extraordinary book. Such a figure indicates that Swift's humor is to some degree a-historical, the persons and paradigms of the story having significance for each generation of readers. The use of different generic modes in *Gulliver's Travels* presumably attracts different kinds of readers, depending on a preference for satire, travel, utopian literature, science fiction, roman à clef, the fantastic, and so on. This manifold richness is the touchstone of a "classic."

Yet some would claim that the importance of *Gulliver's Travels* derives from its historical specificity as part of the Tory reaction to Sir Robert Walpole's Whig oligarchy of the 1720s—the "Robinocracy," as it was called. If topical significance is expanded to culture as a whole, the importance of the work lies in its record of a struggle between the shaping forces of British society, between emergent "moderns"—utilitarian, urban, and mercantile—and humanist "ancients"—conservative, intellectual, and anti-scientific. The contrasts between Gulliver as a "modern" and Swift as an "ancient" will be developed throughout this study. In short, *Gulliver's Travels* is a major document in the European struggle between progress and reaction, a battle of ideas of far greater magnitude than any fought with weapons. This importance is at the center of the following chapters, yet there is a greatness in *Gulliver's Travels* that transcends time and place.

Twentieth-century anthropology and the social sciences have recognized the relativity of cultural history in the evolution of peoples. Consequently, the neoclassical concept of the "universality" of truths underlying change seems rather rhetorical, if not redundant. Nevertheless, within the contingencies of history there are continuities as well as changes. Swift and his French translator, the Abbé Desfontaines, differed on a related issue. Though the translation of 1727 softened some of Swift's satire to suit the polite taste of the French, Desfontaines remains an interesting and sympathetic early critic of Swift. On one point, however, they disagreed. In the preface Desfontaines notes, "[I]t is clear that this book was written not for France, but for England, and that what it contains of direct and particular satire does not touch us" (Williams, 83). Swift replied, "If then, the works of Mr. Gulliver are calculated only for the British Isles, that traveller must pass for a very wretched writer. The same vices and the same follies reign everywhere, at least in all the civilised countries of Europe, and the author who writes only for a town, a province, a Kingdom, or even a country, so far from deserving to be translated, does not even deserve to be read" (Williams, 87). Some satire, like Swift's *A Tale of a Tub* (1704), runs the risk of sinking under its topicality, but in this letter Swift claims that the particular contemporary allusions to political life are representations of more general abuse.

This claim is often found in satire and can seem like special pleading or an expression of neoclassical distaste for the personal satire of the lampoon—having your cake and eating it. As historical scholarship has identified many topical references in *Gulliver,* Swift's words might arouse skepticism. But this would miss what is most important and exciting. Michael Foot, a prominent British politician, author, and former leader of the Labor party, recommended "that everyone standing for political office in Dublin, the United States or London, should have a compulsory examination in *Gulliver's Travels."* Mind, society, and civilization evolve, but there is a marked continuity in public life, from the ancient world to today. The same corruption, hypocrisy, ambition, and self-delusion appears, whether in ancient Athens, Imperial Rome, Georgian London, or Republican Washington.

John Hawkesworth, an early editor of Swift, recognized that abuse of language is part of this corruption, and it is demonstrated in *Gulliver's Travels.* Commenting on Gulliver's account of recent European wars to his Houyhnhnm master (IV.v.248–51), Hawkesworth notes, with great percipience, "It would perhaps be impossible, by the most laboured argument or forcible eloquence to show the absurd injustice and cruelty of war as effectually, as by the simple exhibition of them in a new light: with war, including every species of iniquity and every act of destruction, we become familiar by degrees under specious terms" (Williams, 153). Swift's plain style counters the cant of "specious terms" of public euphemism and shocks us out of our complacency. This is the great power and truth of *Gulliver's Travels,* and it is needed now as much as ever.

3

The Critical Reception

Since publication in 1726, Swift's best-known satire has occasioned delight and dismay, sometimes in the same reader. The early, hostile response was shaped largely by middle-class values of benevolism, refinement, and politeness. In the eighteenth century, *Gulliver's Travels* was both decried and defended, with the attackers gaining ground by sheer weight of number rather than force of argument. In the nineteenth century, the attackers won the field, while in the twentieth century polarized views reappeared simultaneously, but on shifted ground of academic debate rather than prejudice.

What caused such vociferous differences? Parts I and II of *Gulliver's Travels,* the voyages to Lilliput and Brobdingnag, the remote lands of tiny people and giants, delighted readers of all ages, particularly youngsters, and these two parts were appropriated to become an illustrated "children's classic." The various voyages of part III—to Laputa, Glubbdubdrib, and elsewhere—have always been regarded as lesser achievements, a view that will be challenged in the course of this study. It is part IV, however, the voyage to the land of the Houyhnhnms, the rational horses, that has occasioned at times near hysteria. The early extremes consist of reactions to the comedy and satire, to Swift's humor;

reactions to the critique of Walpole's Whig administration, to Swift's politics; reactions to Swift as the mad misanthrope, identifying the satirist with his persona, Lemuel Gulliver.

As Arbuthnot wrote to Swift on 5 November 1726, "*Gulliver* is in everybody's hands."[1] "From the highest to the lowest it is universally read," John Gay reported on 17 November, "from the Cabinet-council to the Nursery." "That countenance with which it is received by some statesmen, is delightful," observed another of Swift's friends, Alexander Pope, on 16 November. This early correspondence contains a witty playfulness of tone and anecdote that also appeared in the correspondents' writings in verse and prose, drawing on *Gulliver's Travels* for its humor. Swift's friends also gave voice to a qualm that reverberated through the eighteenth century and beyond. Pope hinted that "some indeed think it rather too bold, and too general a satire." Gay echoes Pope's words, "the Satire on general societies of men is too severe," continuing, "Those of them who frequent the Church, say, his design is impious, and that it is an insult on Providence, by deprecating the works of the Creator." Yet, characteristic of the early reception, Gay adds as a compensation, "Notwithstanding I am told the Princess hath read it with great pleasure."

The political satire against the Whigs in parts I, II, and III of *Gulliver's Travels* prompted an anonymous *A Letter from a Clergyman to his Friend* (1726), which generally accuses Swift of "rancor," "malice," and "envy" toward the government and offers an encomium on Walpole, "This Great Man . . . the wise Director of the public Affairs." The irony of this is that the clergyman defender of government sounds exactly like Gulliver before the King of Brobdingnag, and thus lays himself open to the charge Swift made on 17 November 1726 in a letter to his friend Mrs. Howard, mistress of the Prince of Wales: "I am not such a prostitute flatterer as Gulliver; whose chief study is to extenuate the vices and magnify the virtues of mankind, and perpetually din our ears with the praises of his country in the midst of corruptions, and for that reason alone hath found so many readers" (*Correspondence*, 3:187). Conversely, the Duchess of Marlborough, a one-time enemy of Swift but by the 1730s at odds with the Whig court, rejoiced in the political satire: "Dean Swift gives the most exact account of kings, ministers, bishops and the courts of justice that is possible to be writ."

The aspect of Swift's satire that provoked a continuing reaction, well beyond the period of Whig oligarchy, was "the nature of man" question. William Warburton, in *A Critical and Philosophic Enquiry into the Causes of Prodigies and Miracles* (1727), saw that this went to the roots of society and civilization: "Ancient Philosophy," he says, gives us "due Veneration for the Dignity of *human nature,*" which Christianity adopted, "our divine Master made it the Foundation of his Religion." Such optimism is threatened by sceptics like Swift, who, according to Warburton, take their philosophy of egotism from La Rochfoucauld and Hobbes, presenting human nature as "base *cowardly, envious,* and *a Lover of its self.*" Samuel Richardson writes in *Clarissa* (1748) that the "abhominable Yahoo story" came from "the overflowings of such dirty imaginations" that debased "the character of human nature, the character of creatures made in the image of the Deity."

Surprisingly, one of the roundest condemnations of Swift and *Gulliver's Travels* came from someone who had purported to be a friend, John Boyle, fifth Earl of Orrery, in *Remarks on the Life and Writing of Dr. Jonathan Swift* (1752). For Lord Orrery, although among Swift's works "there are those that delight and improve me," on the other hand, "There are some pieces that I despise, others that I loath." As an example of the latter, Orrery touches on the voyage to Brobdingnag, but reserves his strongest condemnation for Houyhnhnmland. There, "Swift has indulged a misanthropy that is intolerable . . . we are disgusted, not entertained . . . in painting Yahoos he became one himself . . . the voyage to the Houyhnhnms is a real insult upon mankind." Orrery goes one step further than his contemporaries and accuses Swift of sadism: "Swift takes pleasure in giving pain." Less sensationally, the key to Orrery's critique lies in his repeated use of the word *delicacy*—Swift's "want of delicacy and decorum," as he puts it. The eighteenth century redefined this term to mean fineness of feeling, the basis of the culture of sensibility that grew out of refinement and politeness. In outward action a gentleman was recognized by "benevolence," while inward being was characterized by "delicacy." In

Orrery's circumlocutionary phrasing, Swift "too frequently forgets that politeness and tenderness of manners, which are undoubtedly due to human kind."

Polite literature should lead to improvement, "in piety or benevolence," according to James Beattie in his *Essays on Poetry and Music as they Affect the Mind* (1776), which is lacking in Swift. More forcefully, in his *Dissertations Moral and Critical* (1783), Beattie attacked the fourth voyage as "an absurd, and an abominable fiction," abounding "in filthy and indecent images," representing "human nature itself as the object of contempt and abhorrence," which went against the "benign dispensations of Providence."

Swift was not without defenders. Unfortunately, one of these, Patrick Delaney in his *Observations upon Lord Orrery's Remarks . . .* (1754), contrived to interpret the Yahoos as "in effect a panegyrick upon the human frame." He also failed to see that the inconsistencies in the Houyhnhnms could be part of Swift's irony. Deane Swift, Swift's cousin and biographer, went directly to the sentimental heart of Swift's critics in *Essay upon the Life, Writings, and Character of Dr. Jonathan Swift* (1755): "these mighty softeners, these kind pretenders to benevolence, these hollow charity-mongers." Deane Swift invokes the language of orthodox Christianity in Swift's depiction of the sin and depravity of humankind's postlapsarian nature, an approach that is strongly argued in the twentieth century by R. M. Frye. Defending Swift against charges of misanthropy in *Gulliver*, George Monck Berkeley questioned the benevolists' automatic assumption of the natural and innate "dignity of human nature" (*Literary Relics*, 1789). Ignoring providential arguments like Beattie's and acknowledging individual acts of virtue, Berkeley champions Swift as a satirist interested in revealing vice and corruption, thereby offering a moral corrective, not the despair and hatred of misanthropy.

Among the strongest of Swift's supporters are two early editors who both prefixed a "life" of the satirist to their editions of Swift's work—John Hawkesworth in 1755 and Thomas Sheridan in 1784. Sheridan goes straight to the point and indicates Swift's method in the fable of the Yahoos and Houyhnhnms: "The design of the author, in the whole of this apologue, is, to place before the eyes of man a picture of the two different parts of his frame, detached from each other, in order that he may the better estimate the true value of each, and see the necessity there is that the one should have an absolute command over the other." Without reason, Sheridan argues, man "would be degraded below the beasts of the field." In the Houyhnhnms are collected "all the virtues, all the great qualities, which dignify man's nature." With some qualification, many still read *Gulliver's Travels* in this way. Of great importance in Sheridan's approach is his insistence on criticism recognizing the literary mode of Swift's writing. Is "mankind so stupid," he asks, "as in an avowed fable, to stop at the outside, the vehicle, without diving into the concealed moral, which is the object of all fable? Do they really take the Yahoo for a man, because it has the form of a man; and the Houyhnhnm for a horse, because it has the form of a horse?"

Hawkesworth's comments on *Gulliver* contain the kernel of what was to become one of the leading principles of aesthetic theory in the twentieth century. Defending Swift against those who charge him with a "wanton imagination" in the creations of Lilliput and Brobdingnag, Hawkesworth writes: "When human actions are ascribed to pygmies and giants, there are few that do not excite either contempt, disgust, or horror. To ascribe them therefore to such beings, was perhaps the most probable method of engaging the mind to examine them with attention, and judge them with impartiality, *by suspending the fascination of habit, and exhibiting familiar objects in a new light*" (emphasis added). In these last phrases Hawkesworth anticipates the concept of *ostranenie* in Viktor Shklovskii and the controversial use of *Verfremdungseffekt* by Bertolt Brecht. *Ostranenie* is usually translated as "defamiliarization," and *Verfremdungseffekt* is well known as the "alienation effect," as "making strange," or "estrangement." Throughout *Gulliver's Travels* contemporary England is "made strange" in the representations of Swift's "defamiliarizing" satire. Hawkesworth's sophistication is well above his most enlightened contemporaries. In a passage too long to quote here but touched on in chapter 2 of this study, Hawkesworth considers the discussion of war in Houyhnhnmland. He examines how we become inured to the "specious terms" that conceal violence and elicit our acquiescence. Swift's depiction strips off "the veil of custom and prejudice." Today the technological language of warfare occludes the atrocities of scientific barbarism.

The breadth of Hawkesworth's vision here is markedly at odds with the narrow moralism of the benevolists. A great exception is Henry Fielding. Though within *Tom Jones* (1749) Fielding champions the benevolist ethic of the Earl of Shaftsbury, particularly in Tom's debate with the Old Man of the Hill (Bk. VIII, ch. xv), his own generosity of spirit embraced the comedic lineage of his contemporary. "Fill my pages with humor," Fielding says—invoking the names of Aristophanes, Lucian, Rabelais, Shakespeare, Cervantes, Molière, Marivaux, and Swift—"till mankind learn the good nature to laugh only at the folly of others, and the humility to grieve at their own" (Bk. XIII, ch. i). But Fielding's liberalism, combined with earthy laughter, drew censure from puritanically polite figures like Richardson. In society and culture the body was clothed and conducted according to elegance and propriety, and mention of bodily functions was anathema. The Rabelaisian use of excremental images as humor, which Swift inherited, brought down the fury of the nineteenth century on the satirist's head.

Nineteenth-century attitudes went to an extreme. In *An Analytical Enquiry into the Principles of Taste* (1805), Richard Payne Knight implies an absolute division in readership: "[T]he *Travels of Gulliver,* with which I have known ignorant and very young persons, who read them without even suspecting the satire, more really entertained and delighted, than any learned or scientific readers, who perceived the intent from the beginning, have ever been." Following Hawkesworth and Sheridan, in 1814 Sir Walter Scott edited an annotated edition of Swift's works, which was reissued in 1824. Scott provides much sensitive and detailed comment, but his biographical approach furthered the Swift mythology. For all his own gifts of imagination as a novelist of worldwide influence, Scott took a literal view of the Yahoo—"so loathsome a picture of humanity." Though aware of the fictive mode and of utopian traditions, Scott does not see any inconsistency in Swift's judgment but accounts for his "malicious . . . execration" as "incipient mental disease" and "universal misanthropy." Criticism disappears and libel takes its place in a culturally powerful figure like Francis Jeffrey, the editor of the *Edinburgh Review*. In 1816 he wrote of Swift as "profligate and unprincipled . . . despicable as a politician, and hateful as a man." In the same context Jeffrey adds that Swift was "the greatest and most efficient *libeller* that ever exercised his trade."

That reason, judgment, and argument should be so vehemently astray indicates that Swift's satire was a real source of fear—for all the rejection, it was still working. This is apparent in the most notorious attack of the century. Thackeray was influenced by Fielding, but he lacked his breadth of vision. In *English Humourists of the Eighteenth Century* (1851), Thackeray acknowledges Swift as "giant and great" and the humor of *Gulliver's Travels* as admirable—except for the Yahoos. From a psychoanalytical viewpoint, the context Thackeray discusses—that of the Yahoo ejecting excrement on Gulliver—is revealing. Thackeray quotes, "almost stifled with the filth which fell about him," and then insists that this is a fitting analogue for the reader's experience. The "filth" is "Yahoo language: a monster gibbering shrieks, and gnashing imprecations against mankind—tearing down all shreds of modesty, past all sense of manliness and shame; filthy in word, filthy in thought, furious, raging, obscene." Such extremity could be taken only one step further, and that was done by George Gilfillan in his 1816 essay "Satire and Satirists." He insists that "Swift is not a satirist, but a minor Satan."

Nineteenth-century discourse on society, mind, and body was sanitized, both literally and metaphorically, as is precisely the case in a bizarre piece of Swift criticism. In *A History of the Reign of Queen Anne* (1880), John Hill Burton claims that "in an age of decorum like the present . . . we have managed to cleanse ourselves of a vast load of impurities" that makes offensive satire redundant. This "cleansing" is analogous to "sanitary science" in the worlds of anatomy and physiology. In the domestic sphere, "the sanitary engineer is replacing the scavenger and nightman." Pressing the analogy again, Burton writes, "some sanitary philosopher will do more in the cause of cleanliness and health than the immortal taunts of the greatest of our satirists." Yet out of the depths of the nineteenth-century mind arose psychoanalysis, and contemporary commentator Norman O. Brown claims

Swift as a Freudian visionary.[2] More traditionally, nineteenth-century critic J. Churton Collins, though agreeing with the notion of Swift's misanthropy, recognized a relationship between Swift's scatology and the orthodox Christianity expounded by the Church Fathers, a view developed in the twentieth century by R. M. Frye (1954).[3] In the early 1980s, Carol Fabricant showed that excremental imagery reflects not so much Swift's mind as his inescapable Dublin environment, animal and human.[4]

Swift was not entirely rejected by the nineteenth century. William Hazlitt spoke out against the prejudice of Jeffrey: "It is, indeed, the way with our quacks in morality to preach up the dignity of human nature, to pamper pride and hypocrisy," whereas in *Gulliver's Travels* Swift attempts "to tear off the mask of imposture from the world" (*Lectures on the English Poets,* 1818). Yet scholars have to search hard to find a voice of sane discrimination when it comes to the Yahoos and Houyhnhnms. The honorable exception is Thomas Tyler in a letter to the *Academy* (1883), where he argues for an ironic presentation of a mock utopia with calculated extremes of bestiality and reason. Tyler sees this as an "expression of . . . fundamental pessimism," which is arguable, but his view is arrived at by observation and judgment, not the hysteria of his contemporaries.

The twentieth century witnessed the passing of the private scholar and the public sage and the demise of belles lettres, which were succeeded by the growth of universities and the rise of English studies. Canons of scholarly impartiality and historical accuracy prevailed in the teaching of, and research into, English literature. Swift studies benefited considerably from academic specialism. Between 1962 and 1983, Irvin Ehrenpreis wrote a monumental three-volume biography; in 1959 Louis Landa produced several studies on Swift's relationship with the Anglican Church in England and Ireland.[5] The leading twentieth-century authority on science and literature, Marjorie Nicolson, produced seminal studies on *Gulliver's Travels* in 1937. The serious study of sources for *Gulliver* was begun by William A. Eddy in 1923, while the question of political allusions has engaged scholars such as Sir Charles Firth (1938), Arthur E. Case (1978), W. A. Speck (1983), J. A. Downie (1984), and F. P. Lock (1980) in a continuing debate throughout this century.[6] The insights accruing from such knowledge will be applied in the chapters that follow.

In spite of this progress, a major aspect of the Swift mythology has persisted. Preceding centuries identified Swift with Gulliver as a "misanthrope." With modern Freudian literary analysis the misanthropist was transformed into the neurotic. The same assumption prevailed—Swift was Gulliver. Whereas nineteenth-century reactions derived from evident bias, psychoanalysis applied its own methodology. A work of art—*Gulliver's Travels*—was accorded the same status as a patient's dream or free association during therapy. Psychoanalysis thereby fulfills its own fantasies by confirming the assumption that *Gulliver* is a neurotic fantasy, frequently relying on unsubstantiated biographical inference. The facility of finding any neurosis whatsoever calls the value of such an approach into question. For example, one psychoanalyst finds not only coprophilia but psychosexual infantilism, eroticism, zoophilia, sodomy, voyeurism, sadomasochism, and both mysophilia and mysophobia.[7] This is not to condemn psychoanalytical criticism. Edmund Wilson's renowned essay, "Dickens: The Two Scrooges," in *The Wound and the Bow* (1941), for instance, added a profound dimension to the study of Dickens. Paradoxically, the Freudian view most often cited is that of Norman O. Brown, who sees Swift as visionary rather than neurotic. In his analysis of Swift's "excremental vision," Brown acclaims the satirist for his revelation of "the universal neurosis of mankind," the "extensive role of anal eroticism in the formation of human culture" (Brown, 172).

Source study, identifying Swift's use of conventions of travel and satire, was followed by a major advance that countered the basis of psychoanalysis. The concept of the mask, or persona, differentiated Swift from his creation. It is difficult now to imagine discussion of Swift's satires without the mask, as it is a fundamental technique: a draper in *The Drapier's Letters,* economic projector in *A Modest Proposal,* modern "enthusiast" and hack in *A Tale of a Tub,* and so on. In the last-named work, Swift's major early achievement, he spelled out his use of this technique. In "The Author's Apology," added to *A Tale of a Tub* in 1709, Swift explains, "the author personates the style and manner of other writers" in "what they call parodies." *Persona* is Latin for "mask," and *personates* means "acting" in seventeenth-century English. In popular entertainment today we have "impersonators." Swift's satires extend the notion of parody of literary style to mimicry of character, both as person and writer—pamphleteer, projector, traveler, etc.

Identification of Lemuel Gulliver as Swift's ironic mask is the first step in an interpretation of the work as a satire. But the practice of reading *Gulliver's Travels* as a realist novel persisted, applying standards of Jamesian rigor. Consequently, discussion of seeming inconsistencies in Gulliver's fiction prevailed over that of the consistency of Swift as satirist, instead of vice versa. Though Gulliver is closer to a fictional character than any of Swift's other personae, fiction is nevertheless part of the satire. Swift's satirical fable masquerades as travel literature. To explore the duality of *Gulliver's Travels,* and the dialectic between Gulliver and Swift, is to take a comprehensive approach, since everything is determined by this interrelationship. The all-encompassing question concerning readerships will be discussed at the close of this study.

As part of an elitist satirical strategy, Swift created a readership divided by the ability to recognize the irony of his work. By the midtwentieth century another division, in an academic readership, took place. In 1974, James L. Clifford categorized the two sides of the debate as the "hard" and "soft" schools of interpretation.[8] To summarize here, the "soft" reads the *Travels* for comedy, satire, and irony. In this reading, Gulliver, the Yahoos, and the Houyhnhnms are satirized for their obtusity, absurdity, and grossness. Gulliver is self-deluded, and the Houyhnhnms represent a false utopian ideal. (In this, the "hard" school sees the "soft" school as ignoring the tragic, serious aspect of Swift's work by overexaggerating the comic. In the "hard" school, the Houyhnhnms represent a true ideal, and Gulliver is alienated by despair. Clifford also touches on the gradations of opinion between extremes.) The "soft" school draws on the history of ideas, situating Swift in the "nature of man" debate, and exonerates the satirist placing the text against the context of Christian concepts of pride and facile benevolist idealism. Sometimes it appears that Swift is ideologically appropriated to support the conservative, if not reactionary, beliefs of the critic and his class. Alternatively, the "hard" school tends to bring a contemporary consciousness to a reading of *Gulliver*, as if it were Swift's. The "soft" school re-creates a humanist readership, while the "hard" school re-creates Swift as a modernist. "Soft" school readings minimize the emotional and imaginative range of the work, while the "hard" school finds next to no place for the humor. Objective criticism needs to account for what happens when we adopt, or fail to adopt, certain habits of reading, and the predispositions that follow. C. J. Rawson (1973) warned of the "rigidities" of mask criticism, and his influential work derives from the theoretical openness of "hard" school criticism.[9]

With great panache, imaginative range, and intellectual rigor, Rawson has been foremost in his comparative studies of Swift and modern writing, from Joseph Conrad and Kafka to Bernard Malamud and Wallace Stevens. Philosophical questions of epistemology, close to Gulliver's experience of languages and learning, are explored in relation to the history of ideas by W. B. Carnochan (1968).[10] Everett Zimmerman (1983) and Nigel Wood (1986) apply the radical approach of modern theorists such as Michel Foucault and Jacques Derrida.[11] A post-Saussurean reading of Gulliver as a re-creation of the reading process rather than Swift's persona is presented by Alain Bony (1973).[12] Anticipating what has become a postmodernist preoccupation with the indeterminacy of meaning, articles by Terry Castle (1980) and Grant Holly (1979) focus on the multiple possibilities of signification in the textuality of *Gulliver*.[13] A recent edition of *Gulliver's Travels* by Christopher Fox in a series titled Case Studies in Contemporary Criticism, edited by Ross C. Martin, contains, in addition to the text, five essays written from different contemporary theoretical perspectives. These are feminism, new historicism, deconstruction, reader-response, and psychoanalysis.[14] Edward Said (1984) has appealed for the necessity of taking historical perspectives on Swift's work, and historians like Betrand Goldgar (1976) and W. A. Speck (1983) have made valuable contributions in this area.[15] These various approaches have, however, erected another duality: the positivist gains of historical inquiry and the postmodernist fascination

with indeterminacy and contradiction that risk the self-canceling negativity of deconstructive approaches. A dialectical method will not
resolve antithetic viewpoints but show their origin in the retroactive
significance that history creates.

A READING

CAPT. LEMUEL GULLIVER
Splendide Mendax. Hor:

Frontispiece to George Faulkner's 1735 edition of *Gulliver's Travels*.

4

The Opening Satirical Frame

This "opening satirical frame" refers to the prefatory material of George Faulkner's 1735 Dublin edition, the frontispiece of that edition, and the opening pages of the voyage to Lilliput. The "closing satirical frame" of chapter 10 refers to both the last three chapters of the voyage to the Houyhnhnms and the frame of history that intervenes between today's audience and Swift's contemporary readership.

To avoid identification and prosecution for his anti-Whig satire, Swift took great pains to exclude himself from the original opening frame in what became the first edition, published in London by Benjamin Motte in 1726. In on the subterfuge, Pope reported to Swift, who had arranged to be back in Ireland, that the manuscript of *Travels into Several Remote Nations of the World,* by Captain Lemuel Gulliver, had been anonymously dropped from a Hackney carriage at the door of Motte's publishing house. With the manuscript was a letter from Gulliver's supposed cousin, "Richard Sympson," suggesting financial arrangements for publication. As Swift did not have the opportunity to correct proofs, not only was Motte's edition full of misprints, but the publisher had toned down parts of the satire. After protests, most of the misprints were corrected for the second edition, but the censorship remained until Faulkner's Dublin edition. It was for this publication that Swift supplied the prefatory "A Letter from Capt. Gulliver to his Cousin Sympson." It seems reasonable to conclude that the engraved frontispiece portrait of Gulliver with the inscription *"Splendide Mendax"* (Magnificent Liar) was added with Swift's approval, since he was on hand in Dublin to oversee corrections and additions. There is general, if not total, agreement among scholars and critics that Faulkner's 1735 edition, the third volume of Swift's *Works,* represents the closest we can get to Swift's original intentions.

The 1735 opening frame consists of the following: a frontispiece and the old title page, both identifying the author; an "Advertisement"; "A Letter from Capt. Gulliver to his Cousin Sympson"; "The Publisher to the Reader"; "Contents"; a map showing Lilliput and Blefuscu; chapter I of "A Voyage to Lilliput" begins. What Swift added to the 1726 edition were probably the inscription *"Splendide Mendax"* for the frontispiece portrait, the letter to "Sympson," and the "Advertisement." Thus with Faulkner's edition Swift added considerably to the satire of the opening frame, in terms of Gulliver's social identity, personal character, and literary personality. The details add up to a specific profile in direct antithesis to that of Dean Swift.

"Lemuel" is a rare forename outside of *Gulliver's Travels.* This is not surprising, since it is buried away in only two references in the Old Testament, in Proverbs 31.1 and 4: "The words of King Lemuel, the prophecy that his mother taught him"; "It is not for kings, O Lemuel, it is not for Kings to drink wine." *Lemuel* is Hebrew for "consecrated to God." Some forenames can broadcast strong social signals, particularly of religious and racial provenance—for example, names like Emanuel, Mohammed, and Aloysius. Who, in the seventeenth century, would ransack the Bible for a name like Lemuel? The answer is obvious. As God's chosen people the Puritans went to the Old Testament to name their children after the ancient Israelites: the more obscure the name, the greater the testament to pious familiarity with Holy Scripture.

The suggestive ironic overtones of the name *Gulliver* have long been recognized. It is an English surname, as indicated in "The Publisher to the Reader," but it also carries satirical connotations.

Gulliver is gullible, and some gullible readers believed that the *Travels* were a real account. Though the etymology is obscure, since the sixteenth century the noun *gull* has meant a "dupe," while the verb *to gull* means "to cheat." The action of plays like Ben Jonson's *The Alchemist* (1612) and *Volpone* (1607) are described as "gulling plots," the gullers working on the gulls.

Splendide Mendax derives from Horace's *Odes* (III.xi.35), but this source has little application to *Gulliver's Travels*. It was occasionally a humanist practice to lift a quote and apply it to different contexts, and this is likely what Swift did. The satirical convention of the lying voyager had been long established within the Menippean tradition, since Lucian's *True History*. Lying voyagers were not simply purveyors of the tall story, the self-evidently fantastic. At one extreme were fantastic voyages, at the other accounts of supposedly real travels whose authors were led to overinsist on their veracity.

Paradoxically, such defensive protestation becomes deconstructive, calling into question the very thing it insists on. In *News from the East Indies* William Bruton writes, "In this . . . discourse, I have tied and bound myself to speak only truth, though it seems incredible or hyperbolic; and, if I should any way swerve or stray from the truth, there are living men of good fortune . . . who are able and ready to disprove me" (in the miscellaneous *A Collection of Voyages and Travels,* 1745). The phraseology and diction seem calculated to suggest that the writer cannot be certain of maintaining the distinction between documentation and imagination. Presumably, he intended to claim that there were fellow voyagers who could testify to the truth of his record. Unfortunately, his expression suggests the reverse. In comparison, as the contemporary reader of *Gulliver's Travels* opened the first pages, he encountered specific social, and blatant literary, signals that pointed to satire. Picking up the Latin tag of *Splendide Mendax,* the educated reader would be predisposed to expect satire, whereas the uneducated reader would assume that here was another account of exotic travels.

While Swift made his satirical intentions crystal clear in the 1735 edition, they are also in evidence in the 1726 edition. In Motte's original preface, "The Publisher to the Reader," "Richard Sympson," as editor, gives details of Gulliver's background. The captain has retired to his home county of Nottinghamshire from Redriff, or Rotherhithe. Though Gulliver is associated with this county, his family apparently came from Oxfordshire, and, "Sympson" adds, "I have observed in the Church-yard at *Banbury,* in that County, several Tombs and Monuments of the *Gullivers*" (xi). Why bother with this extraneous detail? The editor's gloss helps—"Banbury: a town famous for its Puritanism" (309). Further notes are provided confirming the continued existence of the Gulliver tombstones and the likelihood of Swift having come across them in 1726. So the Puritan hint in the name *Lemuel* is identified further. Banbury is doubly emphatic, since it was established within the tradition of satire in the portrayal of Puritans. The character Zeal-of-the-Land Busy in Ben Jonson's *Bartholomew Fair* (1614) is described in the dramatis personae as "a Banbury man." Busy's Banbury provenance is repeated four times in the first act, including the phrase "your Banbury man." Jonson uses an established label, and the fame of his play ensured its continuation. *Bartholomew Fair* was the first play Charles II asked to see after the defeat of the Puritan revolution, at his Restoration in 1660. These details of Gulliver's Puritan background will be added to those of the opening pages, shortly.

Not long before Swift came out with his book, a plagiarized work, titled *A New Voyage to the East-Indies* (1715), was published, the author using the fictitious name "Captain William Sympson." In giving Gulliver's friend the name "Richard Sympson," Swift presumably wished to suggest an association (or perhaps he misremembered the first name?) with literary fraud, thus further undermining the seeming factuality of the text. Swift compromises things still further when "Sympson" suggests that Gulliver "is a little too circumstantial" with excessive detail (xi) immediately after Sympson himself has been just that. Swift loves to generate multiple ironies, above all in the extensive "A Letter from Capt. Gulliver to his Cousin Sympson."

By 1735 Swift was known as the author of a satire, *Gulliver's Travels.* When the work was new, in 1726, Swift exploited the extremes of readership. To offer an analogy—today some people believe that soap-opera characters are real people; from a psychological point of view, they intensify their viewing by maintaining this belief. Conversely, in the 1720s, there were those cognoscenti who not only recognized and enjoyed the satire of politics but who also recognized the satire of a genre *and its readership*. These could relish others' naïveté and their own intellectual superiority.

The notoriety of *Gulliver* had by 1735 diminished the shock of the new. The original frontispiece was naturalistic, simply bearing the legend "Captain Lemuel Gulliver of Redriff Aetat. suae 58." Paul Turner's edition reprints the engraving but adds the inscription "*Compositum jus, fasque animi, sanctosque recessus / Mentis, et incoctum generoso pectus honesto*" ("a heart rightly attuned towards God and man; a mind pure in its inner depths, and a soul steeped in nobleness and honour," Loeb translation). Swift adapts these pious sentiments from Persius's second *Satire* (ll. 73–74)—a far cry from the "Magnificent Liar" of 1735, which, with the "Letter," provides a revised satirical, rather than realistic, emphasis. Ostensibly, the "Letter," which reads as if it were added seven months—rather than nine years—after publication, elaborates on the problems of publishing *Gulliver* that are touched on in the "Advertisement." But the letter has the important effect of developing the Swift persona in several ways. As both voyager-author and Puritan-reformer, Gulliver is rounded out as a character. But Gulliver is unaware of the irony by which readers recognize the mask in the literary artifice of the ulterior satirist—Jonathan Swift.

At the opening of the "Letter," Gulliver claims to have advised the most famous English voyager-explorer, William Dampier, to correct his *A New Voyage round the World* (1697). There is evident conceit here, if not a little arrogance, following the opening touch of irascibility in Gulliver's tone. Then, in the midst of discussion of Queen Anne's reign, Gulliver interjects, "as it was not my Inclination, so was it not decent to praise any Animal of our composition before my Master *Houyhnhnm*" (xxxv). This is odd. Who are these mysterious and strange-sounding Houyhnhnms? Swift never refers at all to horses in the table of contents. New readers would be drawn by the mystery, while old hands re-reading could enjoy the mock obliquity. "Master" implies the human, but the use of the word "Animal" to describe humans complicates matters. The oddity is continued in Gulliver's curious phraseology, "you have made me *say the thing that was not*" (xxxv). After a reference to "*Yahoos*" (xxxvi), things begin to come grotesquely clear: "Have not I the most Reason to complain," Gulliver asks, "when I see these very *Yahoos* carried by *Houyhnhnms* in a Vehicle, as if these were Brutes, and those the rational Creatures?" (xxxvi). He goes on to explain that "so monstrous and detestable a Sight" was the chief motive for his retirement to Nottinghamshire. The candid reader can draw only one conclusion: the Yahoos are human, the Houyhnhnms are horses, and Gulliver is a little crazy, since everyone knows that horses are animals and that in creation only man has a portion of reason.

Gulliver's vanity and self-righteousness appear in his disappointment that in what according to him are the seven months since publication, the reformist intentions of his *Travels* have not corrected "every Vice and Folly to which *Yahoos* are subject" (xxxvii). Swift uses a favorite satirical technique at this point. Gulliver records that, "I desired you would let me know by a Letter, when Party and Faction were extinguished; Judges learned and upright; Pleaders honest and modest" (xxxvi), and continues, itemizing eight more abuses. The satire uses a dialectical irony. Two voices are heard saying the same words, but meaning different things. By this stage of the opening satirical frame we are aware of Gulliver as a mask being used ironically. In this listing the voice of Gulliver is naive. How real is an understanding of vice that believes it can be completely cleared up in seven months, simply by pointing it out?

At this stage, Gulliver's understanding of society and human nature is limited by the absoluteness of self-deluding ideals. Swift's voice testifies to the very thing Gulliver fails to see—the intransigence of vice and folly, not things as they should be but things as they are: ignorant and dishonest judges; the false, exaggerated claims of litigants; and so on. Gulliver goes mad because he has not converted England to Utopia. Swift, in his sanity, recognizes that the ideal of such human perfectibility is itself the sin of pride. As in this example, Swift sometimes speaks *through* the mask and sometimes partly *removes* it. In the first case the voices are evenly balanced in ironic tension, in the second Swift allows a heavyweight irony to send up Gulliver, as in the following passage, when he ensures that readers recognize Gulliver's utopianism: "[S]ome of [the Yahoos] are so bold as to think my Book of Travels a meer Fiction out of mine own Brain; and have gone so far as to drop Hints, that the Houyhnhnms and *Yahoos* have no more Existence than the Inhabitants of *Utopia*" (xxxviii). The "Letter" closes with the misanthropic Gulliver rejecting his family, the Yahoos, and "visionary Schemes," retreating to his stable to confer with his "degenerate" Houyhnhnms.

Swift creates an ironic disjunction between what is intended by Gulliver and how we actually respond, between how Gulliver sees himself and how we see him. In the "Letter" our awareness of Gulliver's conceit, arrogance, and craziness is quite beyond his own. That disparity is the source of the dialectic that is the mainspring of the satire, when Swift chooses to bring it into play.

As the reader contemporary with Swift turned to the first page of *Gulliver's Travels,* there in visual and verbal form was another part of the dialectic, that of the pedestrian and the wondrous, the fictive and the factual, as indicated by the first of the maps opposite the opening page of chapter I. Arthur E. Case argues that the inaccuracy of the maps derives from the engraver's ineptitude, not from Swift's burlesque of mapmakers' accuracy to add to his satire (Case, 54). Yet the fact that the maps were reused in the Faulkner edition seems to indicate that Swift was not bothered by them. Whatever its inaccuracies, the first map is a perfect analogue for Swift's literary art. The factual "Dimens Land" (Van Dieman's Land) and Sumatra appear, and then the islands of Lilliput and Blefuscu, rendered with cartographic reality. Yet up against the coastline of Sumatra are "Hogs I" and "I Good Fortune," namely Hogs Island and the Isles of Good Fortune, or The Fortunate Islands. Motte's engraver renamed Circe's island (Aeaea), as Hogs Island, after the fate of Odysseus's companions, which was particularly remembered in Plutarch's dialogue of the Greek wanderer with one of the hogs, entitled *Gryllus.* The Fortunate Islands derive from classical mythology and often arise in Renaissance discussion of terrestrial paradises. They were eventually identified with the Canary Islands. Evidently, the map parallels the frontispiece with its give-away inscription.

In contrast to the book's preliminary pages, chapter I begins with a solid, factual, biographical account of Gulliver. In these seemingly neutral details that serve to complete the social identity of Gulliver, Swift manages to combine seemingly plain description with subtle satirical allusion. "My Father has a small Estate in *Nottinghamshire;* I was the Third of five Sons." So begins *Gulliver's Travels*. Gulliver returned to Newark in Nottinghamshire, though the family originally had strong Banbury connections, in Oxfordshire. Puritan notoriety and Banbury were legendary. At the beginning of the seventeenth century, however, recalcitrant Separatist groups of Puritans began to organize around the border villages of Gainsborough, Scrooby, and Bawtry, just twenty-odd miles from Newark.[1] A Baptist faction within this community established contact with the dreaded Anabaptists on the Continent. The whole Scrooby congregation eventually decamped to Leyden and notoriety. Thus Gulliver is a noninheriting, middle son of lesser Puritan gentry who had moved from Banbury to a known area of Puritan faction in Nottinghamshire, to which the disillusioned visionary retires.

Gulliver was unable to remain at Emmanuel College, Cambridge, because of his father's straightened fortunes. Though it had acceded to the Royalist, Anglican Restoration, Emmanuel was the foremost Puritan college of seventeenth-century England. Having to make his way in the world, Gulliver turns from humanist studies at Cambridge and takes up an apprenticeship with a surgeon, his father only intermittently supporting him. His goal is to become a ship's surgeon. Going from humanism to the "mechanick" arts of navigation and mathematics, Gulliver has utilitarian foresight in planning his career as seaman. This is furthered by a long period studying "Physick" at Leyden, to prepare himself as ship's surgeon on long voyages. As a dissenter, Gulliver would not have been allowed to study at the Royal College of Physicians. Leyden University was a Reformation foundation in a country that had always given refuge to English Puritan exiles. Furthermore, the city of Leyden provided one of the great bogeymen of the sixteenth and seventeenth centuries. The "King of Sion," Jan Bockelson of Leyden, otherwise known as Jack of Leyden, was abhorred throughout Europe. Jack of Leyden joined the

Anabaptist millenaries at Münster in 1534 to inaugurate an apocalyptic New Jerusalem, which turned into a grotesque bloodbath. Swift groups "Dutch Jack" with other reformist fanatics at the end of section VI of *A Tale of a Tub*. What Gulliver presents as a set of neutral facts Swift knows will have far from neutral resonances.

After initial voyages, Gulliver returns to London and sets up in practice as a physician and marries the daughter of a hosier from Newgate Street. These last details are often taken as a satirical side thrust at Daniel Defoe. Defoe was originally a hosier and married an heiress. He was imprisoned in Newgate after spending the dowry. Of greater significance is the fact that Defoe was a nonconformist.

With these details assembled from the first page and earlier in the opening satirical frame, a distinct social profile takes shape. The argument here is at odds with the common view that Gulliver is the completely average, ordinary, pedestrian Englishman of the period. There is a sense in which this is true, and it is necessary for a degree of flexibility in Swift's adopted persona. It has been argued by E. A. Block that Swift deliberately made Gulliver the middle son from (very roughly) the middle of England, with a middle-class father, having a middle-class religion and receiving a middle-class education.[2] To maintain this leveling averageness, there is a considerable blurring of social, geographic, and educational edges. The profile presented above has greater clarity and critical application.

To summarize, Gulliver comes from lesser Puritan gentry down on their luck and has to turn from the pursuits of a leisured or professional gentleman to the urban, mercantile, utilitarian world of flourishing nonconformity. Gulliver will make his way in the thriving new middle-class world. Not once does Swift use the word *Puritan*. Any reader of the day would have picked up the social signals. As a historian, W. A. Speck is one of the few critics who has focused on such detail. He sees Gulliver as a Whig, in contrast to Swift's Country Tory ideology (Speck 1983, 67). This is certainly true, but Gulliver's Whiggism is part of a whole conspectus of values, all of which by 1726 were inimical to Swift. These values congregate around one of the words at the center of Swift's worldview: *modernism*. In the opening satirical frame and thereafter, Gulliver intermittently embodies the values, ideas, and activities of "modernism"—self-reliance, practicality, and profit. In the emergent new world of scientific empiricism, religious dissent, and mercantile wealth, the moderns could realize their destiny. God's blessings were identified with the economic individualism of the middle classes: industrious and utilitarian, the world lay all before them.

5

Lilliput: The Beginning of a Dialectic

By *dialectic* is meant an intellectual process involving opposites. In *Gulliver's Travels* the dialectic is between the factual and the fictive, truth and lies (or delusion), the pedestrian and the wondrous. However bizarre or fantastic, there is always a dialectical relationship between what Gulliver finds in his travels and what can be found in the past and present history, politics, and society of England. The parallelism and contrast between the strange lands Gulliver visits and home is felt directly or indirectly throughout. Above all, the controlling dialectic is that between the created and the creator: author-Gulliver and his book, finally invalidated and displaced by author-Swift and his book.

For Swift to sustain *Gulliver's Travels* he has to exploit the midpoint between the extremes of the dialectical mode. That midpoint lies in the mediatory mentality of Gulliver, the plainness of his imagination, in which Swift finely balances the credible and the incredible. When we encounter the unbelievable, it is made believable by the ordinariness of Gulliver—he is surprised and bemused, alarmed and bewildered, as we would be. As readers we share with him a distanced perspective on past actuality. This ordinariness has led to the view of

Gulliver as an Everyman figure and of the *Travels* as Swift's satire against humankind—a partial truth. Swift ultimately uses general satire to validate more particular social and political ideology.

SWIFT AND GULLIVER

The dialectic of *Gulliver's Travels* is laid out diagrammatically in figure 1. The scheme brings out graphically the antithetic contrasts between Swift and Gulliver, with the top four characteristics, listed at number 1, reflecting the situation at the opening satirical frame, and with the last group, listed at number 4 (madness/sanity etc.) anticipating the closing satirical frame. As we have seen, Gulliver comes from a Puritan background. Swift does not directly confront this in doctrinal terms but strongly hints at it with cumulative social detail. By the end of the seventeenth century the wide spectrum of religious dissenters from the doctrine and practice of the established Anglican Church were known as nonconformists, after their refusal to conform to the Act of Uniformity, enacted in 1662, which expelled priests who had not been ordained by bishops. In his "Letter . . . to his Cousin Sympson," Gulliver makes clear that the record of his travels was intended not just as an entertaining account but as a work of moral and spiritual reformation.

Swift, on the contrary, was a lifelong upholder of the orthodoxy of Anglicanism. His satire derives from a neoclassical tradition of learned wit going back to Lucian and Menippus, with Erasmus's *In Praise of Folly* and Sir Thomas More's *Utopia* as leading examples, in Tudor humanism. This lineage is in part acknowledged on Glubbdubdrib, with More's inclusion of the sextumvirate, the group of six spirits. In the scheme of figure 1, Swift's "satire on humankind" is opposed to Gulliver's "reformation." This is a large issue that will be examined in chapters 9 and 10 of this study, but it needs to be raised here as it constantly features in critical discussion of the *Travels*. A common critical approach takes the view that Gulliver is an ordinary representative Everyman. Further, when the societies he visits are satirized, any topical political or social allusions are intended to be exemplary of more uni-

Figure 1. The Dialectic of *Gulliver's Travels*

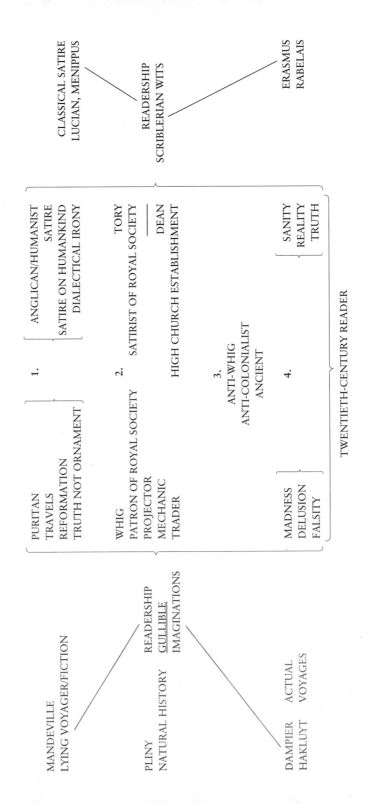

versal folly and vice. It follows that when Gulliver himself is the object of satire, he is merely the vehicle for the nature of humankind in general. All of this is undoubtedly true, but it is not the whole truth. Ultimately, Gulliver represents a number of characteristics that embody "modernism." Swift uses religious and moral commonplaces about pride and reason to elicit readership consensus that reinforces the contemporary social particularity of his satire against an emergent middle class. Swift's satire is ideological, not impartially Olympian. The difficulty is that a number of commentators have shared Swift's conservatism and have therefore automatically considered Swift in his own terms, or acceptable approximations of such. In the dialectical approach adopted here, an attempt will be made to see both Gulliver and Swift in the objective perspectives provided by history. The ideological awareness of modern literary theory helps to clarify such a reappraisal.

Chapter 1 of this study included a brief outline of the skeptical reaction to the Renaissance celebration of man in such a figure as Montaigne. Pyrrhonic skepticism, founded on relativity of values, undermined the proud claims for man as a rational animal. For Pyrrho the question of what we can know or not know cannot even be raised since all evidence is inadequate. Such beliefs worked their way into the French literary culture of the seventeenth century, particularly satire. The species homo sapiens as an object of ridicule appeared in the satire of such poets as Sieur Des Barreaux, Mathurin Regnier, and most famously, Boileau, whose "Satire 8" provided the impetus for the most distinguished example in English. John Wilmot, Earl of Rochester, most notorious of the Restoration rakes, libertine and man of wit, was also a gifted poet, in spite of chronic alcoholism, venereal disease, and an early death at age thirty-three, in 1680. Here are the opening lines of his most famous poem, "A Satyr against Mankind":

> Were I (who to my cost already am
> One of those strange prodigious Creatures *Man.*)
> A Spirit free, to choose for my own share,
> What Case of Flesh, and Blood, I pleas'd to weare,
> I'd be a *Dog,* a *Monkey,* or a *Bear.*

Lilliput: The Beginning of a Dialectic

Or any thing but that vain *Animal,*
Who is so proud of being rational.

Gulliver would prefer to be a horse, yet he embraces a higher rational-ism. Swift's recorded doubts about the validity of the definition of man as rational animal, and its application to *Gulliver's Travels,* have in large part led to the view of the work having an affinity with satires against humankind.

Section 2 of figure 1 lists some of the various ways in which Gulliver and Swift identify themselves in the course of the voyages. Before the King of Brobdingnag, Gulliver espouses a fulsome kind of 1720s Whiggism. Swift was always a High Church Tory in religion, and his Toryism in politics was shaped by the Country Party Toryism of the 1690s, which Robert Harley, later the Earl of Oxford, brought with him into power from 1710 and which was championed by Swift in the *Examiner* papers of that period. The decline of revolutionary Whig idealism into the politics of opportunists and the oligarchy of the 1720s served to confirm Swift's position. As dean of St. Patrick's, Dublin, Swift at least had a decent position within the church of Ireland, in comparison with his earlier living at Laracor, where he had been isolated within a largely Presbyterian community.

Discussion of the Royal Society, founded in 1660 for the fur-therance of experimental science, will be necessary when considering Gulliver's visit to the academy of projectors in Lagado (part III), but suffice it to note here Gulliver's patronage of the society in contrast to Swift's satire on science. About to visit the academy, Gulliver lets slip, "I had my self been a Sort of Projector in my younger Days" (III.iv.177). The word *projector* in this period carries strongly experi-mental, utilitarian, and practical connotations, associated with empiri-cal science. When Gulliver defends himself against an attack of wasps in Brobdingnag, he keeps some of the stingers, which are "an inch and a half long, and as sharp as needles," and eventually presents them "to *Gresham College*" (II.iii.101–2), the establishment of the Royal Society in London. Gulliver's rather detached empirical observation through-out the *Travels,* and his direct, simple style, reflects the Royal Society's dependence on correspondents, travelers, and explorers and its recommendation of a nonrhetorical prose. It is characteristic of Gulliver that when he has killed two marauding rats—an episode nightmarish for the reader—he then precisely measures their tails, "two yards long, wanting an Inch" (II.i.84). Similarly, when pelted by hailstones as big as tennis balls, he weighs and measures them and calculates mathematically their proportion to those in Europe (II.v.109). Finally, on Lilliput, Gulliver signals his affinity with the artisan class by "Having a Head mechanically turned" (I.vi.50)—that is, he shows an ability for practical construction—and he makes a table and chair.

The central positioning of the third group in the scheme of figure 1—anti-Whig, anti-colonialist, and ancient—draws attention to one of the long-standing problems in the study of the text. Namely, sometimes Gulliver's views and those of Swift are identical, and for some this appears to introduce to the writing an unacceptable inconsistency. On Lilliput Gulliver becomes a vehicle for the satire of court Whigs of the 1720s, whereas on Brobdingnag his Whiggish views are the object of satire. Almost sixteen years earlier, Swift had formulated his critique of the Whigs on Queen Anne's change of ministry to the Tories. In the twenty-ninth paper in the *Examiner* series, for instance, Swift specifically identifies the corruption of the Whigs in aligning themselves with the Low Church nonconformists, not to mention Atheists and Anabaptists. Throughout all of his career in Ireland, Swift attacks England's colonialist policies. Toward the close of the *Travels*, though Gulliver had in effect expressed colonialist views on Brobdingnag, Swift gives him one of the most powerful anti-colonialist diatribes ever penned, too long to quote fully, but too powerful to pass over without an example: "Here commences a new Dominion acquired with a Title by *Divine Right*. Ships are sent with the first Opportunity; the Natives driven out or destroyed, their Princes tortured to discover their Gold; a free Licence given to all Acts of Inhumanity and Lust; the Earth reeking with the Blood of its Inhabitants: And this execrable Crew of Butchers employed in so pious an Expedition, is a *modern Colony* sent to convert and civilize an idolatrous and barbarous People" (IV.xii.302–3).

"Modern" is a key concept for Swift, and by and large Gulliver is a truly "modern" representative throughout the *Travels*. Yet on the

Island of Sorcerers, in the voyage to Glubbdubdrib, Gulliver is vouch-safed a magical vision of figures from classical antiquity and British history in which the moderns come off very poorly in comparison with the ancients. This will be examined in chapter 8. Once again Gulliver is a vehicle of satire in a passage strongly reminiscent of Lucian. Swift can be at his most playful and teasing when he deliberately narrows the ironic gap between voices—a characteristic that would have delighted fellow members of the private Scriblerus Club Swift formed with Pope, Arbuthnot, and others for witty dining and satirical scheming, but that can be frustrating for readers today. In figure 1, the problem of readerships is laid out in dialectical terms—Scriblerian wits opposed to gullible readers, with some reminders of the materials in chapter 1 of this volume. At the bottom of the diagram we find ourselves, the twentieth-century reader; this complex issue will be looked at in the final "closing satirical frame."

LILLIPUT AND GULLIVER

Returning to Lilliput, Swift's basic technique is to ground the opening of each of the four parts of *Gulliver's Travels* in the solidity of the real geographical, social, and historical world. Gulliver as a solid historical person appears against the setting of late-seventeenth-century commercial London. Gulliver provides nautical details of latitudes, lands, ship, and crew as he sets off, recounting details as if keeping a ship's log. The tone is dispassionate, even when shipwreck occurs, and Gulliver shows a mariner's discipline in keeping a grasp on facts. Gulliver records wading ashore: "The Declivity was so small, that I walked near a Mile before I got to the Shore, which I conjectured was about Eight O'clock in the Evening. I then advanced forward near half a Mile" (I.i.5). Precision of space and time is vigorously observed as an empiricist's article of faith, creating credibility and authority—and the grounds for contrast in the dialectic of the pedestrian and wondrous.

Within a page the exhausted Gulliver is captured by a nation of little people no more than six inches high. But the prisoner's attitude hardly changes at all. The past tense establishes some rhetorical distance. Though Gulliver "was in the utmost Astonishment" and felt "excessive Pain" (I.i.6) from the arrows, the tone is dispassionate and descriptive, not dramatic and emotional. By avoiding psychology and stressing situation, Swift creates an imaginative space in the medley of fact and fiction, the credible and incredible. We may or may not be like Gulliver, but in the circumstances we would react in the same way. Swift grounds fantasy in the reality of comparative proportion, in which the link between the real and fantastic, London and Lilliput, is constantly implicit. Gulliver is secured by "the King's Smiths [who] conveyed four score and eleven Chains, like those that hang to a Lady's Watch in *Europe,* and almost as large" (I.i.12). It hardly matters whether the reader has observed the precise thickness of such watchchains. The naturalness of the simile gives the reader imaginative confidence in Gulliver's account.

In contrast, Swift's usual satirical techniques include the literalization of the metaphorical and the logic of absurdity. Both compromise the reader's imagination and reason by turning an unacceptable social reality into an outrageous fantasy. For example, in *A Modest Proposal,* the economic principle of "domestic consumption of domestic products" is linked to the notion of landlords exploiting tenants as "devouring" the people. The literal and metaphorical ideas suggested by *devour* are turned into the economic phantasmagoria of cannibalism, the marketing of year-old babies as nutritious food. Swift wrote *The Drapier's Letters* in opposition to a proposed minting of new coinage—"Wood's halfpence"—that would have flooded Ireland and debased the value of existing currency. Working from a false premise concerning the weight of the new coins, at one point the satire "logically" works out the physical necessity of horses and carriages carrying cash to conduct ordinary business. In *Gulliver's Travels,* Swift does the reverse, particularly in Lilliput. There observation of proportion establishes plausibility in the way that detail succeeds upon detail, creating a whole world that is both real and fantastic. In the example from *The Drapier's Letters,* Swift applies an approximation of geometric progression to challenge the reader's grasp of economic realities, whereas the *Travels* bases the reader's experience in Gulliver's relative imaginative restraint, since almost everything he says or does is concerned with practicalities. Linking imagination to the evidence of the senses underwrites fantasy.

We are pulled up short by the logic of this imaginative engagement at the end of the first voyage when Gulliver safely returns with some of the Lilliput livestock that have survived the journey: "The rest of my Cattle I got safe on Shore, and set them a grazing in a Bowling-Green at *Greenwich,* where the Fineness of the Grass made them feed very heartily, although I had always feared the contrary" (I.i.68). Anticipating the second voyage, proportions are inverted. Solid actuality, however, compromises imagination. The imaginative free play on Lilliput is displaced by fantasy now superimposed on reality. Greenwich and a trim bowling green are real; miniaturized cattle are creations of fantasy. The reference to presenting fashionable exhibitions that would have outclassed popular "shows" (like that on Brobdingnag) heightens the humor, not the reality. Ineluctable fact now challenges the fictive. The reverse was the case on Lilliput, where we suspended the distinction between truth and lies, fact and fantasy.

When Gulliver captures the Blefuscu fleet and pulls it across the channel to Lilliput, do we allow our imaginative engagement with the strategy to be disturbed by its sheer impossibility? The Blefuscu ships are nine feet long, and Gulliver claims to have dragged "with great Ease . . . fifty of the Enemy's largest Man of War after me" (I.v.38). On Brobdingnag, recalling this and other actions recorded in Lilliputian chronicles, Gulliver bemoans, "Posterity shall hardly believe them" (II.i.77). Again, when first captured by the Lilliputians, Gulliver admits to being tempted "to seize Forty or Fifty of the first that came in my Reach, and dash them against the Ground" (I.i.8). But, given the proportions, he could have held only two or three in each hand. Even if "fifty" is taken as hyperbole, it belies the care Swift takes elsewhere to be "credible." More seriously, one of Gulliver's entertainments at the court of Lilliput calls his veracity into question. He claims to have made a raised platform of "two Foot and a half square" (I.iii.26) from his rather outsized handkerchief, upon which a troop of the king's best horses, "Twenty-four in Number" (I.iii.26), undertook military exercises, attacking, retiring, and the like. The Emperor's largest horses are four-and-a-half inches high, so the military horses would have been a little lighter than these draught animals, and shorter for speed. Simple calculations demonstrate that each horse would have barely had room to turn around in, let alone undertake military maneuvers. These examples point up Swift's strategy of providing sufficient detail for the imagination to work, and enough just here and there to subvert that engagement. Ironically, in illustrations of *Gulliver's Travels* both these scenes are commonly depicted, with silently revised dimensions.

Gulliver as "*Splendide Mendax*" is hinted at in these instances in contexts that, when looked at cursorily, seem to be merely examples of the inventive, playful imagination children delight in. Elsewhere, part I of the *Travels* is best known for its political satire in which the voyager has a largely expository role as a somewhat naive recorder of what he sees and hears, the *ingenu* vehicle of larger social criticism. Even so, Swift takes some pains to lay the foundation of what is to grow by part IV into one of the major, and most contentious, aspects of the satire: Lemuel Gulliver's pride. On securing the Blefuscu fleet Gulliver is "created . . . a *Nardac* upon the Spot, which is the highest Title of Honour among them" (I.v.39). Shortly after this Gulliver recounts that being a Nardac, "the highest Rank in that Empire," he is exempt from "Offices . . . looked upon as below my Dignity" (I.v.42). In defending his reputation against the Treasurer, Gulliver boasts, "I had the Honour to be a *Nardac,* which the Treasurer himself is not; for all the World knows he is only a *Clumglum,* a Title inferior by one Degree" (I.v.53). Gulliver forbears from physical retaliation against the impeachment he is about to receive as much out of pride in his title as out of moral principle (I.vi.60). That ethical confusion is to grow throughout the work as Swift directs his satiric focus on Gulliver rather than on politics and society at large.

LILLIPUT AND POLITICAL ALLEGORY

Chapters III and IV of the voyage to Lilliput contain some of the notorious satire that was immediately interpreted as part of the wave of propaganda against Walpole associated with the publication of the

Craftsman, an oppositional journal. In chapter III Gulliver describes the game of rope dancing: "This Diversion is only practised by those Persons, who are Candidates for great Employments, and high Favour, at Court" (I.iii.24). Sometimes ministers are expected to show that they have retained their skills, and Gulliver's enemy, Treasurer Flimnap, "is allowed to cut a Caper on the strait Rope, at least an Inch higher than any other Lord in the whole Empire" (I.iii.25). Another "diversion" is that of the game of leaping and creeping over a stick held by the Emperor, or a minister, which is rewarded according to greatest agility by blue, red, or green silk threads, now worn by most members of the court.

In chapter IV, Gulliver's friend Reldresal, the Principal Secretary of Private Affairs, outlines the contemporary political situation of "two mighty Evils: a violent Faction at home, and the Danger of an Invasion by a most potent Enemy from abroad" (I.iv.34). Two political parties dominate, the Tramecksan and Slamecksan, named respectively after the high and low heels of their footwear, by which they identify themselves. The Low Heels are favored by the Emperor and occupy all the positions of administration and government. The ruler even signals his political affiliation: "[Y]ou cannot but observe . . . that his Majesty's Imperial Heels are lower at least by a *Drurr* than any of his court; (*Drurr* is a Measure about the fourteenth Part of an Inch)" (I.iv.35). The High Heels outnumber the Low Heels and—unfortunately for the Low Heels—seem to be favored by the heir to the throne, one of whose heels is plainly higher than the other, causing a hobble in his gait.

The other source of contention is the neighboring island state of Blefuscu, "the other great Empire of the Universe" (I.iv.35), with which Lilliput has been engaged in hostilities for generations. Division derives from the Lilliputian custom of breaking their eggs at the smaller end, while the Blefuscans insist on the ancient practice of breaking eggs at the larger end. The present Emperor of Lilliput's grandfather cut his finger while conventionally breaking an egg at the big end, whereupon the Emperor's father issued an edict commanding the reverse practice. From thence arose an internal division between Big-Endians and Little-Endians. Schism, rebellion, and warfare ensued, with Blefuscu championing the Big-Endians and offering refuge for exiles.

There is a general acceptance that Swift is engaged in political allegory here, but there is considerable variance of opinion on precise details. Few would disagree that the High and Low Heel parties refer to the Tories and Whigs. The Prince of Wales was said to have laughed out loud at the description of the heir to the throne hobbling on high and low heels. The prince patronized Tory Country party politicians whose disaffection from practical power politics had drawn them to an idealized amalgam of old Whig and Tory principles. (Swift's shifting political allegiances will be examined along with those of Gulliver in the presence of the King of Brobdingnag in the next chapter.) Parallel to these political affinities are Tory patronage of the High Church (established Anglicanism) and the Whig party's association with the Low Church (nonconformity). The satire of the Little- and Big-Endians is thought to refer to Reformation controversy concerning administration of the bread and wine at the Eucharist. Aside from this doctrinal specificity, the egg represented Christianity as the adopted symbol of resurrection. Allusions to the Emperor of Lilliput's ancestors are usually taken to refer to Henry VIII and the English Church's break with Roman Catholicism. The main critical controversy concerns the court games of the Lilliputians—rope dancing, leaping, and creeping.

Early this century Sir Charles Firth seems to have resolved the details of the issue.[1] Believing that Swift began writing the voyage to Lilliput in 1714 and completed it after 1720, Firth, writing in 1919, interpreted the topical allusions as belonging to the reigns of both Queen Anne and George I. Within this framework, Gulliver's pissing on the royal palace to put out a fire and the Empress's deep offense could be interpreted as Anne's offense at the religious satire of *A Tale of a Tub*. The Treasurer Flimnap's agility in the gymnastic rope dancing makes contemporary reference to Sir Robert Walpole. With Flimnap/Walpole as key, the allegory can be unlocked and the High Heels, Low Heels, Big-Endians, and Little-Endians seen in appropriately contemporary or historical terms from the vantage point of the 1720s. Interpretation, however, can seem as much a question of ingenuity as of historical scholarship. Does the searching of Gulliver correspond to searches for Jacobites? Does Gulliver's flight to Blefuscu equal Bolingbroke's flight to France in 1715? Sometimes Reldresal is identified with Lord Carteret, who dealt leniently with *The Drapier's Letters* in 1724.

After decades of acceptance, Arthur E. Case challenged Firth's findings. Lilliput now referred to the latter half of Queen Anne's reign. Allusions to the 1720s appear in Brobdingnag. For Case, Gulliver's fall from grace in Lilliput represents the fall of the Tory leaders, Harley and Bolingbroke, in 1708. The search of Gulliver and the lengthy inventory alludes to the Whigs' attempt to smear Harley with the treason of one of his subordinates. Gulliver's conditional release refers to Harley's return to power in 1710. It continues: the capture of the Blefuscu fleet and Gulliver's firefighting refer to the treaty of Utrecht; Gulliver's eventual impeachment alludes to the victorious Whig attack on Harley and Bolingbroke in 1715 (Case, 70). The debate continues with W. A. Speck picking considerable holes in Case's method, argument, and facts as he goes on to suggest that if attention is paid to the dates for the first voyage (1699–1701), there is a case for paralleling the inventory of Gulliver's belongings with the Partition Treaty of 1700, which concerned the claimants to the Spanish succession; Gulliver's release with the Act of Settlement, by which Parliament continued the royal succession; and Gulliver's impeachment with that of four Whig lords for signing the Partition Treaty.[2]

Speck continues, carefully building his case, but acknowledges that Swift might well have been deliberately ambiguous. Caution was necessary, punishment could be severe. Motte, the first publisher, changed the colors of the silk threads of the leaping-creeping game to purple, yellow, and white, from blue, red, and green, respectively the colors of the Order of the Garter, the Order of the Bath, and the Order of the Thistle. Walpole was made a member of the first in 1726. In recent years, J. A. Downie and F. P. Lock have returned to the problem, each stressing somewhat opposed positions.[3] Though Downie amended Case's work and suggested that the satire was more general than commentators allow, he could not go as far as Lock, who found that Swift's satirical targets were on the whole general paradigms and typical examples. This view returns us to Swift's objection to the Abbé Desfontaines's censorship: "The same vices and the same follies reign everywhere."

The hallmark of great satire, it could be argued, is that in spite of topical bite, it takes on a wider meaning when absorbed into history. For example, the dystopian and satirical writings of George Orwell in *1984* and in *Animal Farm* are now read at a distance from 1948 and the Stalinist USSR. Yet subsequent totalitarianism has given these works a visionary relevance in addition to their original significance. Comparably, the rope dancing and leaping and creeping games are topical and metaphorical. Inventive flexibility prompts imaginative application to later times. The rope dancing, leaping, and creeping of those seeking or holding onto high office can be seen daily in contemporary politics.

Another visionary, at least for Marxists, was the Tudor humanist Sir Thomas More, author of *Utopia* (1516). The Irish poet W. B. Yeats said of Swift, he "haunts me: he is always just round the next corner."[4] As Swift was to Yeats, so More was to Swift, and he appears in part III. More's *Utopia* haunts *Gulliver's Travels.* Chapters III and IV of the voyage to Lilliput develop a satirical analogy with post-Revolution England and post-Reformation Europe. In chapter VI contemporary Lilliput is compared to a utopian past. There is a structural comparison with *Utopia* here, since the political, social, and economic failings of England and Europe are outlined in book I of *Utopia,* while the second book represents in antithetic contrast a hypothetical ideal. Just as More provided an important prefatory letter after writing *Utopia,* so Swift copies him in supplying his "Letter" in 1735.

In More's *Utopia* there is neither money nor private property, and food is freely distributed. Therefore few laws are needed. Government is by an elected hierarchy of councils and officers, republican in structure, but with an elected prince. Everyone is literate, everyone works, everyone learns agriculture and a craft, thereby forestalling the division between urban and agrarian life. Work, rest, and leisure are balanced, and a national health system looks after welfare. Social distinctions are minimized by limited, simply made clothing. Gold is scorned. A learned class of clerics maintains a Deistic religion, but tolerance is an essential principle, providing each individual believes in immortality. The unit of the household is closely regulated. Marriage is monogamous, pragmatic, and eugenic, not to say anti-romantic. Diplomacy and warfare are all carried out with the assumption that only the power-mad few seek destructive battles. Utopia is a communistic mean between the extremes of European luxury and beggary, vice and asceticism, destruction and division.

Many details of the Lilliputian utopia derive from More, just as More writes in the shadow of Plato's *Republic*. Plutarch's *Life of Lycurgus* was unique as it depicted the realized utopia of ancient Sparta—there are touches of this in Lilliput, but it is of greater significance in the land of the Houyhnhnms. Utopia as a hypothetical contrast to the actual is immediately taken up by Gulliver: "There are some Laws and Customs in this Empire very peculiar; and if they were not so directly contrary to those of my own dear Country, I should be tempted to say a little in their justification" (I.vi.45). The ironic inflection of "my own dear Country" jars with the earlier tone of the analogy and adds a satirical dimension to Gulliver by anticipating the Whiggish stance of the following voyage. Gulliver's account offers an inverted mirror of England.

In Lilliput victims of false accusation are not doubly punished by legal costs, but fully compensated. Ethics are regarded more seriously than material crime. Abuse of ethics—trust, honor, confidence—is graver than appropriation of property. Laws reward the good as well as punish the bad. Moral qualification for office takes precedence over intellectual acumen. Idleness, luxury, and corruption are forestalled by an ascetic and utilitarian education. Although the polity is hierarchic, there is a communal program of welfare and responsibility for all members of society. In the midst of his account, however, Gulliver hastens to remind readers, "In relating these and the following Laws, I would only be understood to mean the original Institutions, and not the most scandalous Corruptions into which these People are fallen by the degenerate Nature of Man," and we are reminded of the "gradual Increase of Party and Faction" (I.vi.47) of chapters III and IV.

Gulliver's Olympian view—there are several allusions to giants of classical literature—reduces all to a scale of petty vainglory that is comically reductive and dismissable. The "delight and terror" of his twelve-mile "universe" (I.iii.29), the Lilliputian Emperor "is taller by almost the Breadth of my Nail, than any of his Court; which alone is enough to strike an Awe into the Beholders" (I.ii.15). The module of greatness deconstructs magnitude. In the following voyage, the reversed dimensions put Gulliver himself at the wrong end of the telescope, and the dialectic widens.

6

Brobdingnag:
Before the Philosopher King

The opening and close of part II of *Gulliver's Travels,* the voyage to Brobdingnag, are particularly patterned and subtle. As in part I, we have the departure from and return to reality, but the emphatic use of parody and suggestive myths mediates the fantastic reversal from pygmies to giants, and giants to humans.

At the opening, Swift makes almost verbatim use of a passage from Samuel Sturmy's *Mariner's Magazine* (1669). For all the travel books in his possession, why was he drawn to this? The answer is that Swift found a parody ready-made and did not have to work up one himself. A monsoon begins, and the passage continues: "Finding it was like to overblow, we took in our Sprit-sail, and stood by to hand the Fore-sail; but making foul Weather, we looked the Guns were all fast, and handed the Missen. The Ship lay very broad off, so we thought it better spooning before the Sea, than trying or hulling. We reeft the Foresail and set him we hauled aft the Fore-sheet" (II.i.74). The nautical terminology continues with such density for nineteen lines. Driven off course, the sailors seek fresh water on an island. Alone, Gulliver sees the others fleeing back to the ship and discovers the reason: "I observed a huge Creature walking after them in the Sea, as fast as he could . . . the Monster was not able to overtake the Boat" (II.i.25). The narrative accounts of a storm and a monster conflate the real and the mythological, but reverse the emphasis. The real description sounds parodic in its excessiveness. The brief account of the giant wading out after the mariners is reminiscent of the *locus classicus,* Virgil's continuation of Homer's story of Polyphemus, one of the Cyclops, blinded by Odysseus. Swift's incidental little satirical dig is that this giant does not see Gulliver, who speedily runs away. Thus Swift makes the real rather parodic and the mythic rather real, reversing the conventional expectations of readership. This is repeated at the close of part II.

As mentioned in chapter 1 of this volume, Gulliver's account of being carried off in his traveling box by a huge Brobdingnagian eagle echoes the similar story by Cyrano that draws on fables like the *Arabian Nights*—all deriving from legends of the giant Roc, or Ruk, bird. This is depicted naturalistically, consistent with the following rescue by the Englishman, Captain Thomas Wilcocks. In this instance, Swift describes the psychological adjustment of Gulliver, whose experience makes him see his situation in Brobdingnagian scale. The humor is controlled by naturalism, yet Swift deliberately undermines this by having Gulliver reflect with inadvertent irony on travel writing. In answer to the captain's hope that Gulliver will publish his story, Gulliver replies: "I thought we were already over-stocked with Books of Travels: That nothing could now pass which was not extraordinary; wherein I doubted, some Authors less consulted Truth than their own Vanity or Interest, or the Diversion of ignorant Readers. That my Story would contain little besides common Events, without those ornamental Descriptions of strange Plants, Trees, Birds, and other Animals; or the barbarous Customs and Idolatry of savage People, with which most writers abound" (II.viii.142–43).

If the "extraordinary" fact of scale in Brobdingnag is overlooked, then Gulliver's misadventures might seem "common events," unlike the sensationalism of other travelers. But that such an impossible oversight occurs where it does ensures that the reader cannot simply respond to the Travels unilaterally, accepting seeming "fact" as unmitigated truth. The possibilities of style and subject that Swift inherited from the instability of genre in the period are always exploited for the ulterior purposes of satire.

Part of Swift's method is to test the attention of the candid reader by the deliberate use of inconsistency. Some instances are glaring, as will be seen below, and some are sedulously placed. For example, Swift inserts a flat contradiction into plain physical detail. In chapter II, Gulliver describes how the farmer carries him to town. Glumdalclitch, the farmer's daughter who acts as nurse, has provided a quilt for Gulliver's traveling box, but he records, "I was terribly shaken and discomposed in the Journey, although it were but of half an Hour. For the Horse went about forty Foot at every Step; and trotted so high, that the Agitation was equal to the rising and falling of a Ship in a great Storm, but much more frequent"(II.ii.88). Later, describing journeys under the patronage of the queen, Gulliver notes that sometimes for a change his box was transferred from a coach to horseback, like that with the farmer. But now the "Agitation of the Horse or Coach" does not trouble Gulliver, "having been long used to Sea-Voyages, those Motions, although sometimes very violent, did not much discompose me" (II.iv.106). A page later, when Gulliver begins to describe the royal kitchen, he desists from further comment, since, "perhaps I should be hardly believed; at least a severe Critick would be apt to think I enlarged a little, as Travellers are often suspected to do" (II.iv.107). These reminders make us keep our guard up.

Swift begins Brobdingnag with a touch of nautical parody, but within lines the story shifts into Kafkaesque fearfulness. Now a pygmy in a land of giants, Gulliver moves from a position of power to powerlessness, playfulness to terror, as death looms all around him. The change of tone makes the effect all the greater, and critical response to parody is relegated by an emotional response to nightmare—yet all this menace merely derives from workers in a field of corn. Gulliver is initially perceived by the farm laborers as a dangerous animal, like an English weasel, a hateful animal to be destroyed. At first the farmer's wife reacts to Gulliver as if he were some kind of toad or spider. It transpires that Gulliver is almost the same size as a Brobdingnagian "splacknuck" (never described, Swift allows our imaginations to work on the less than endearing name). Gulliver's animality begins in Lilliput with his monstrous defecation. Now he is seen as verminous.

Swift's satire works on a level of topical sophistication here, in relation to the development of the microscope, which builds on an earlier analogy of the satirist as moral anatomist. In a famous passage of *A Tale of a Tub,* again using a favorite technique, Swift literalizes the metaphorical. At the opening of *Every Man Out of His Humour* (1600), Ben Jonson's Asper promises revelation of "the time's deformity / Anatomised in every nerve, and sinew." Swift goes one step further. "Yesterday I ordered the carcase of a beau to be stripped in my presence; when we were all amazed to find so many unsuspected faults under one suit of clothes" (section ix). Well-publicized experiments with the microscope provided Swift with literal data he could turn to satirical account.

In describing the Brobdingnagians, Gulliver notes: "[T]he most hateful Sight of all was the Lice crawling on their Cloaths: I could see distinctly the Limbs of these Vermin with my naked Eye, much better than those of an European Louse through a Microscope; and their Snouts with which they rooted like Swine. They were the first I had ever beheld; and I should have been curious enough to dissect one of them, If I had proper Instruments (which I unluckily left behind me in the Ship) although indeed the Sight was so nauseous, that it perfectly turned my Stomach" (II.iv.105).

Lense grinding and production had become so widespread that microscopes were available not only to the professional scientists of the Royal Society, the "virtuosi," as they were somewhat sarcastically called, but to any interested member of the public. Swift wrote to Stella (with Vanessa, one of the two close female friends of his life) proposing the purchase of a microscope. "Shall I buy it or no? 'Tis not the great bulky ones, nor the common little ones, to impale a louse (saving your presence) on a needle's point; but of a more exact sort, and clearer to the sight, with all its equipage in a little trunk that you may carry in your pocket" (*Correspondence,* 1:97). The letter anticipates the fictional metamorphosis that was to take place years later on Brobdingnag, when Glumdalclitch, the young girl emotionally attached to Gulliver— seen as vermin by others—carries him around in a little box on her lap.

A huge sixteen-inch engraving of a louse was one of the illustrations in Robert Hooke's *Micrographia* (1665).[1] Dr. Hooke was the curator of the Royal Society, and his microscope observations of such things as leeches in vinegar, mold on leather, and the head of an ant were presented to early gatherings at Gresham College. In *The History of the Royal Society* of 1667, Thomas Sprat celebrated the microscope as one of the triumphs of the "moderns" over the "ancients," and it is true that the scientific and medical origins of bacteriology and histology arise in these years. Antonie van Leeuwenhoek, an equally distinguished contemporary of Hooke, went one step further and discovered that man himself was verminous. Put more scientifically, Leeuwenhoek discovered under the microscope in human saliva and mucus protozoa. They were described as "little animals," like worms or eels.

The purely scientific discovery serves in Swift's imagination to give even greater force to the anti-benevolist view of the human being as an animal. Obviously, on Lilliput humanity is put under the microscope, and on Brobdingnag Gulliver observes as if looking through a microscope, and is observed in this way by the Brobdingnagians. When the king has three distinguished scholars examine Gulliver, they are like three scientists at the Royal Society called on to examine something being seen for the first time in nature through a microscope: "These Gentlemen, after they had a while examined my Shape with much Nicety, were of different Opinions concerning me. They all agreed that I could not be produced according to the regular Laws of Nature . . . They observed my Teeth, which they viewed with great Exactness, that I was a carnivorous Animal" (II.iii.95). The "scholars" use a magnifying glass. The "Pocket Perspective" (I.ii.23), or small telescope, that Gulliver carries may be seen as a fitting emblem for the first two voyages. It reappeared in a Swift *Intelligencer* paper (number 9) of 1728, lamenting the baleful lack of education among aristocratic youth, "so that if you should look at him in his Boyhood through the magnifying End of a Perspective, and in his Manhood through the other, it would be impossible to spy any Difference."

Thomas Shadwell's *The Virtuoso* (1676), a satirical comedy, is the most protracted literary jibe at contemporary science. "Men of Wit," like Samuel Butler, repeatedly made science the butt of their satire. Those who, like Gulliver, made collections of "curiosities" for exhibition or experiment were a particular target, as in Richard Steele and Joseph Addison's *Tatler* essay for 26 August 1710—"Will of a Virtuoso"—which alludes to "rat's testicles," "grasshoppers," and "vermin." In his poem "Last Instructions to a Painter" (ll.16–18), Andrew Marvell laughed particularly at Hooke's engraving of the louse clinging to a human hair:

> With Hooke, thou, through the microscope take aim,
> Where, like the new comptroller, all men laugh
> To see a tall louse brandish the white staff.

From a scientific point of view such laughter could easily be withstood in the light of the clear advancement of knowledge. Such optimism could extend to the religious view of science, demonstrating the infinite pattern and plenitude of God's creation. Galileo's telescope had discovered infinite cosmic worlds, the microscope discovered *microcosmic* worlds—a word formerly applied to the human being as microcosm. For those who did not share this optimism, the human being as a Renaissance paragon seemed reduced to a mite lost in an infinity of worlds. This was the position of Blaise Pascal, the seventeenth-century mathematician and seeker after religious truth. Though converted by a mystical experience, he was sometimes seized with terror at the animalistic nonentity of man as revealed by science. Pascal looks back to the centuries of Christian Deism and forward to twentieth-century existentialism, not least to the hero of Kafka's story "Metamorphosis," who awakes one morning to find himself changed into vermin.

With Gulliver as part of the summary image of "little odious vermin" (II.vi.126), an intermittent process of reification, invalidation, and alienation takes shape. This part of Gulliver's experience on Brobdingnag is remarkably close to modern theoretical categorization of alienation as powerlessness, meaninglessness, social isolation, normlessness, and self-estrangement.

Initially, Gulliver's physicality on Lilliput seems appropriate, but within the development of the work as a whole something more significant has begun. At first Gulliver as a body is reified by others, then

he feels himself alienated by the bodies of others, and, finally, returning from Houyhnhnmland, he is reified absolutely both in body and
mind when he is invalidated socially and politically by madness. These
concepts will be examined again in the "closing satirical frame" of this
study. Swift uses scale and proportion to defamiliarize, that process of
familiar things seen anew, noted by his editor John Hawkesworth.
Taking this one stage further, defamiliarization of object leads to
estrangement of both the perceiver and the perceived. The difference
between the two is the difference between the playful and the painful,
between comedy and tragedy. The satirical and imaginative range of
Gulliver's Travels includes both. The following contrasting examples
will bring out these dimensions.

Some Lilliputians discover "a great black Substance lying on the
Ground, very oddly shaped, extending its Edges round as wide as his
Majesty's Bedchamber, and rising up in the Middle as high as a Man . . .
it was no living Creature, as they first apprehended for it lay in the
Grass without Motion" (I.iii.27). Gulliver identifies his lost hat. In
Brobdingnag, Gulliver observes a nurse suckling a baby: "I must con-
fess no Object ever disgusted me so much as the Sight of her monstrous Breast . . . It stood prominent six Foot, and could not be less
than sixteen in Circumference. The Nipple was about half the Bigness
of my Head, and the Hue both of that and the Dug so varied with
Spots, Pimples and Freckles, that nothing could appear more nauseous" (II.i.82). Gulliver is physically displayed when forced to become
an entertainment in country shows, before his entry to the court.
Viewed as much as a superior "splacknuck" as a miniaturized Brobdingnagian, Gulliver's antics make human actions comic and ridicu-
lous. Swift is a master at shifting rhetorical perspectives.

At one point, waking from a dream of home in a bedroom three
hundred feet wide, Gulliver has to defend himself in a bloody battle
against rats as big as dogs. Reality is a dream and Gulliver wakes into
nightmare (II.i.83). Yet, shortly, we are laughing at his misadventures
with a dwarf, a monkey, birds, and a frog. Sometimes these shifts follow immediately upon each other. In contrast to the Lilliputian soldiers' laughter, marching beneath a Colossus with monstrous genitals,
rather than Olympian brain (I.iii.28), the court maids treat Gulliver

"like a Creature who had no sort of Consequence" (II.v.111) and undress before him. He experiences horror and revulsion at their magnified physicality. Gulliver then witnesses an execution by decapitation, with veins and arteries spouting blood as high as the fountain at Versailles (II.v.112). In the next paragraph the queen instructs a carpenter to build Gulliver a tiny pleasure boat and a trough for an artificial lake, on which the mariner "would put up my Sail, and then my Business was only to steer, while the Ladies gave me a Gale with their Fans" (II.v.113). We move from estrangement and horror to delightful comic play in three pages. (It is not surprising that, in articles and books, critics often select aspects of *Gulliver's Travels* for particular arguments, since the manipulative strategies of tone and contrast in the work as a whole demand a flexibility of response that challenges the most experienced reader. The contemporary reader of *Robinson Crusoe,* encouraged by the title of Swift's work to expect something similar, must have been quite abashed.)

Analogously, the King of Brobdingnag cannot understand Gulliver, at first believing him to be a clockwork device and then disbelieving the "Story" (II.iii.94) of his misadventures. Court philosophers think Gulliver an inferior carnivore, an "abortive Birth" and settle for "Lusus Naturae" (II.iii.95)—a sport of nature. The comedy and the horror is in that provocative phrase: man not so much "A being darkly wise, and rudely great," as Pope put it in *An Essay on Man,* but man as an amorphous mutation—at worst a contemptible animal, at best the object of sportive ridicule. Gulliver finds himself such as the Whig defender of faith before a philosopher king. When Gulliver first expounds on "the Manners, Religion, Laws, Government and Learning of *Europe*" (II.iii.98), the king seats him on a table in front of a "Salt-seller," anticipating the seasoned propaganda that follows. The king indulgently lifts Gulliver up, stroking him like a pet animal, asking if he were a Whig or a Tory, and observing, "how contemptible a Thing was human Grandeur, which could be mimicked by such diminutive Insects as I" (II.iii.98). Swift turns humanist colloquy to Kafkaesque parable.

A branch of humanist literary culture was the study of ethics and politics combined in rulership. With the Renaissance discoveries this took on importance as new societies and peoples were measured against the polities of antiquity. Much utopian literature reflects on political conduct, paralleling a humanist genre of the Renaissance—the advice to princes, whether Sir Thomas Elyot's *The Book Named the Governor* or Machiavelli's *The Prince*. Much of *Gulliver's Travels* reflects these humanist concerns. As well as his "modernist" bent to collect data for the Royal Society, Gulliver has the humanist impulse to record and exchange knowledge of rulers and rulership. In his various colloquys, societies are described, attacked, and defended, so that considerable sections of the work read like a fictionalized debate.

Gulliver expected "to be a Morsel in the Mouth of the first among these enormous Barbarians," since "human Creatures are observed to be more Savage and cruel in Proportion to their Bulk" (II.i.77). Yet on Lilliput the tiny humans were vicious warmongers, whereas, in spite of the rough exploitation of the farmer, on Brobdingnag Gulliver finds himself before a gentle giant who is a philosopher king. Plato left Syracuse disappointed that Dionysus could not be guided as a philosopher king, but in *The Republic* he expounds the ideal of wise rulers and provides a foundation for European utopianism. On Brobdingnag the powerful monarch displays Socratic reason in confronting Gulliver's Whig chauvinism.

In response to the king's inquiry, Gulliver attends five audiences of several hours each, during which his listener takes notes. Gulliver records only a two-page summary of his panegyric on "the Constitution of an *English* Parliament" (II.vi.121)—the peers of the realm and church, the House of Commons, and the courts of justice. All are presented in an idealized eulogy, a bland mélange of flattery, self-congratulation, and complacency. When *Gulliver's Travels* was published in 1726, Gulliver's statement could be interpreted as a celebration of the post-Revolution, dynastic status quo of George I, the Whig heaven on earth. Clive T. Probyn prints a document from Swift's time illustrating this, *The Third Change . . . to the Grand jury . . . of Middlesex* (1726), by Sir Daniel Dolins. It is a remarkable coincidence that Gulliver's account is virtually a summary of Dolin's fulsome benedictions. The following quote is necessarily typical, as Dolin's style never varies:

> Thro' the Goodness of Divine Providence, and the tender Care and Concern of our most Gracious Sovereign King GEORGE: Thro' the wise and watchful Counsels of our Nobles, and the steady, rigorous, and seasonable Revolutions and Laws of our whole Legislative Body: And, lastly, thro' the prudent, gentle, easy Methods, and unwearied Diligence and Application of our Great Ministers of State, in the Execution of Justice, and Administration of our Publick Affairs at Home and Abroad, with so much Secrecy, so much Despatch, and so great Success and Reputation to our King and Country.[2]

The King of Brobdingnag, having listened to this sort of thing for many hours, offers a devastating critique by Socratic questioning and suggestion. Was qualification of nobility for rule determined by favor, bribery, or class bias? How far is the aristocracy qualified by knowledge of law and religion, or are its members the placemen of patronage? How far does the Commons exploit office by bribery, corruption, and betrayal of public interest? The king spots Gulliver's underestimation of tax and expresses surprise that a wealthy country should be near bankrupt. Swift summarizes, using one of his most crushing satirical techniques, the extended catalogue: "He was perfectly astonished with the historical Account I gave him of our Affairs during the last Century; protesting it was only an Heap of Conspiracies, Rebellions, Murders, Massacres, Revolutions, Banishments; the very worst Effects that Avarice, Faction, Hypocrisy, Perfidiousness, Cruelty, Rage, Madness, Hatred, Envy, Lust, Malice, and Ambition could produce" (II.vi.125).

The king offers his own summary for all that Gulliver has said: ignorance, idleness, and vice qualify legislators; laws are explained, interpreted, and applied by those bent on "perverting, confounding, and eluding them" (II.vi.126). The reality of corruption is the reverse of eulogizing acclaim. The most-quoted lines of *Gulliver's Travels* conclude the king's condemnation, "I cannot but conclude the Bulk of your Natives, to be the most pernicious Race of little odious Vermin that Nature ever suffered to crawl upon the Surface of the Earth" (II.vi.126).

In Gulliver's reaction to this, Swift reverses the satirical technique of the voyage to Lilliput, and the critical focus is on what Gulliver represents. Gulliver becomes the object of satire, whereas on

Lilliput he had largely been the vehicle for satire on what he observed. A succession of vertiginous ironies are played against the mariner-author, now hardly a character at all but an embodiment of outrageous contradictions. In response to the king's charge, he argues, "Nothing but an extreme Love of Truth could have hindered me from conceal-ing this Part of my Story" (II.vii.127). But his earlier misrepresenta-tions hardly derive from "love of truth," which he immediately confirms: "Yet this much I may be allowed to say in my own Vindication; that I artfully eluded many of his Questions; and gave to every Point a more favourable turn by many Degrees than the strict-ness of Truth would allow. For, I have always born that laudable Partiality to my own Country" (II.vii.127). The "Vindication" becomes a self-indictment, as such circumlocution amounts to further distortion and evasion. This is a standard Swiftian technique of damning with praise, particularly self-praise—"Laudable Partiality" is double-edged, as it clearly applies to Gulliver's falsification. Lies are hardly "laud-able." We have witnessed the king's liberal open-mindedness; Gulliver now accuses him of "*Prejudices,*" "*Narrowness of Thinking,*" and a "*confined Education*" (II.vii.127–28)—terms glaringly applicable to himself.

To ingratiate himself with the king, Gulliver offers one of the tri-umphs of "modernism"—the formula for gunpowder. The humane horror of the monarch rejects such destructive power as evil. Such compassion, for Gulliver, derives from "*narrow Principles*" and "*short Views,*" the "*unnecessary Scruple*" of someone ignorant of political sci-ence (II.vii.129). Commentators point up the contradiction between the Gulliver of Lilliput and of Brobdingnag. On Lilliput, Gulliver protested that he "would never be an Instrument of bringing a free and brave People into Slavery" (I.v.40) and refused to help the Emperor in his plans to subdue Blefuscu. On Brobdingnag, Gulliver insists that gunpowder would make the king, "absolute Master of the Lives, the Liberties, and the Fortunes of his People" (II.vii.129)—that is, a tyrant. Some of the satire here is deliberately heavy-handed, as the typograph-ical emphasis in italics indicates, but there is also subtlety.

In the summary describing "the Constitution of an English Parliament" (II.vi.121), Gulliver had outlined the ideals of Old Whig government. Upheld by Swift and inherited from classical models, these ideals comprised the limited, or mixed, polity of king, nobles, and commons; the balance between monarchical, aristocratic, and democratic powers. The revolutionary Whigs grafted this onto the notion of an ancient "gothic" constitution restored after Stuart tyranny to preserve the hard-won liberty of the common man. On Brobdingnag, we witness the ludicrous transformation of the Whig libertarian, Gulliver, into tyrannical absolutist. The philosopher king, however, rules over a factionless utopian society, regulated by a militia that ensures constitutional balance. Gulliver is contemptuous of the utilitarian efficiency of government by common sense and justice free from the *arcana imperii*, the mystification of state machinery. Brobdingnagian science is not contaminated by Aristotelian obfuscation. Laws are simple and few, as in More's Utopia. Literary culture is not overwhelmed by journalistic hacks—the denizens of Grub Street. The history of Brobdingnag resembles that of England and Europe, with "the Nobility often contending for Power, the People for Liberty, and the King for absolute dominion" (II.vii.133), all of which leads to civil war. The King of Brobdingnag had been horrified at the disclosure of a "mercenary standing Army" (II.vi.124) in England. His own domain is guarded by a citizen's militia. Swift shared the common post-Revolution distaste for standing armies as the executive tool of tyranny. A militia was believed to prevent any such absolutism by guarding the balance of power.

Once again Gulliver returns home, and Swift derives hilarious comedy from the traveler at first assuming that his seamen-rescuers are Brobdingnagian giants and his family Lilliputian pygmies. But a darker note has entered into the satire of part II. There is something more disquieting than the satire on party politics and social divisions. Gulliver's spasmodic revulsion, the perception of his animality, and the hinted madness add a psychological dimension to his character and the book as a whole. In Houyhnhnmland, Gulliver's alienation becomes political, but in a different way—which can make *Gulliver's Travels* seem closer to Alexander Solzhenitzyn than to Hogarth, closer to the gulag than to Bedlam.

7

Laputa: England and Ireland

Critics tend to look down on part III of *Gulliver's Travels,* like the Laputians looking down on Gulliver. Contemporary references indicate a preference for parts I and II, with part IV attracting much polemical debate. The complementary nature of scale in Lilliput and Brobdingnag gives an aesthetic satisfaction that perhaps leaves the reader disappointed with the heterogeneous nature of the later voyages. Any compelling critical reason to relegate part III is hard to find. Consider what opinion might be if Swift had not written parts I, II, and IV. The voyages to Laputa, Balnibarbi, Glubbdubdrib, and Luggnagg would surely be regarded as masterpieces of satire, of major significance in Swift's work and in the literature of the early eighteenth century.

There is no evidence that Swift had various satirical materials available and decided to use them up. On the other hand, he did initially reflect on the "Wood's halfpence" affair in Laputa, but withdrew a dangerous passage, which was rediscovered and restored in the 1890s. Adding to the critical issue is the evidence indicating that the "Voyage to the Houyhnhnms" was written before part III but was subsequently placed after it as the final section. Such a sequence suggests an overall conceptual scheme of a satire on humanity—successively political, physical, intellectual, and moral. Alternatively, some suggest that part III can be relished as *satura lanx,* a satirical "mixed dish," according to classical conceptions of the mode. My point of view is a plain one. It is self-evident that *Gulliver's Travels* would be less rich without part III. These voyages add considerably to the work as a whole and offer great imaginative achievements as satire. Many moments—including the Laputian "flappers," the spirits on Glubb-dubdrib, the absolutist court of Luggnagg—are among the most memorable in all of Swift's satire. Further, certain narrative moments serve to focus on issues at the center of Swift's life, thought, and writing. Thus the decision, in organizing this study, to separate the voyages of part III into two chapters: "Laputa: England and Ireland" and "Balni-barbi and Glubbdubdrib: Ancients and Moderns." Swift spent most of his career engaged in thinking about the relationship of England and Ireland; the flying island, Laputa, encapsulates much of this. For Swift, "modernism" infiltrated every area of life—literature, politics, science, and religion. It is directly confronted in Balnibarbi and Glubbdubdrib.

The opening pages of part III suggest that Swift carefully added to an overall pattern concerning Gulliver's material situation and early misfortunes at the outset of his voyages. In his first voyage, he is ship's surgeon and suffers shipwreck. He is forgotten by his terrified crew during his second voyage. On his third, Gulliver mentions that he had been "a fourth Part Owner, in a Voyage to the *Levant*" (III.i.149), a budding mercantilist-trader. Captain William Robinson proposes that Gulliver share the captaincy, have another surgeon beneath him, and take double pay. Delayed in Tonquin, the captain uses Gulliver's experience, sending him off to trade in a new sloop. Gulliver's misfortunes now derive not from nature but from man—pirates. Finally, at the outset of the fourth voyage, Gulliver is captain of the ship and a South Seas trader. But Gulliver's roguish crew mutiny and abandon him on a strange shore. Further contrasts in Gulliver's fate suggest Swift's sense of satiric design.

At the end of the voyage to Brobdingnag, Gulliver had fallen from the skies. Now, coming across the flying island, Gulliver is raised to the skies. The Laputian king is the opposite to that of Brobdingnag. While the philosopher king was eager to learn of other lands and peoples, the Laputian monarch is quite indifferent: "His Majesty discovered not the least Curiosity to enquire into the Laws, Government, History, Religion, or Manners of the Countries where I had been" (III.ii.163). The King of Brobdingnag was repelled by the thought of tyranny, whereas the Laputian ruler "would be the most absolute Prince in the Universe, if he could but prevail on a Ministry to join with him" (III.iii.168). Gulliver's function is now reversed. Formerly verminous physically, and Whiggish politically, he becomes more the neutral observer and recorder, as the satirical focus shifts from him onto the societies he encounters. The flying island maneuvers by magnetic attraction and repulsion, a powerful political metaphor, which is analogous to Swift's satirical maneuvers between the reader and Gulliver from sympathy to rejection.

Swift's technique of contrast is part of the controlling dialectical invention, and to counterpoise the science fiction of the flying island, the material circumstances of Gulliver's predicament are stressed more than in previous voyages. Gulliver lands on an island: "It was all rocky; however I got many Birds Eggs; and striking Fire, I kindled some Heath and dry Sea Weed, by which I roasted my Eggs" (III.i.151). The next day he finds another island, "all rocky, only a little intermingled with Tufts of Grass, and sweet smelling Herbs. I took out my small Provisions, and after having refreshed myself, I secured the Remainder in a Cave, whereof there were great Numbers. I gathered plenty of Eggs upon the Rocks, and got a Quantity of dry Seaweed, and parched Grass, which I designed to kindle the next Day, and roast my Eggs as well as I could . . . My Bed was the same dry Grass and Sea-weed which I intended for Fewel" (III.i.152). Within a short space Swift suggests the dreary repetitiveness, sparsity, and uniformity of the habitat, a perfect backdrop for the appearance of the flying island.

By 1726, literary voyages to the moon had become an extraterrestrial subgenre of travel literature, a distant ancestor of space fiction. Scientists of the day had begun pondering the workability of flying machines. Defoe's *The Consolidator* (1704) draws on both. Swift had an inventive genius for fictive amalgamation. Years before, his old patron, Sir William Temple, had spoken of England as a "floating island," at the mercy of the tide of political opinion. Perhaps elaborating on this hint, Swift synthesizes the by-then conventional literature of travel fantasy with contemporary science and technology. Lucian, Cyrano, and Godwin featured voyages to the moon. Swift combines extraterrestrial destination with the means of getting there—the moon and the flying chariot. Marjorie Nicolson points out a similarity between the manner of Gulliver's ascent to the flying island and the ascent of Domingo Gonsales, the hero of Godwin's *The Man in the Moon.*[1]

Common to moon voyages, travelers express wonder at the dimensions of the heavenly body, its shape, and, of course, its inhabitants. In turn the inhabitants submit the traveler to their bemused inspection. The experience of Gulliver is made consistent both with the convention and with his other voyages, and we are given a comparative account of the milieu and mores, court and customs of Laputa. A particular concern with all extraterrestrial voyages was with the method and means of motion, and this is an extensive preoccupation of Gulliver in his detailed exposition.

Scientific speculation on flying machines in the Royal Society, debated by such figures as Robert Hooke and Sir Christopher Wren, was usually confined to the avian coordinates of feathers and wings, but yet again fact and fiction, science and fantasy overlapped in wilder speculation on flying machines, flying chariots, and aerial ships using such materials as balloon-shaped copper domes. Cyrano preceded Swift with fantastic speculation on magnetism as a means of propulsion. The flying machine in Defoe's *The Consolidator* follows the bird model with wings, but is huge enough to incorporate a great stateroom and is moved by a combustible fuel—prescient indeed. No wonder that conservative disdain usually invoked the myth of Icarus, whose wings melted as he flew too near the sun.

Another classical myth prefigures the modern in the island of Delos among the Cyclades; as recorded by Pindar, it floated until fastened by Zeus, with adamantine chains, to the bottom of the sea. Gulliver perceives "a vast Opake Body" (III.i.152) about two miles high with a flat, shining underside reflecting the sea. Ever resourceful, Gulliver uses his pocket perspective and discovers that the flying island is inhabited by people who control its movement, an ironic contrast to the joke made by the captain at the end of the last voyage in the allusion to Phaeton, fateful charioteer of the sun (II.viii.144). The flying island briefly eclipses the sun, but it does not appear to be a portent, as Gulliver is hoist aloft and rescued.

In the satire on science and politics that follows, Swift develops one of his most effective tropes, the literalization of the metaphorical, but here in a dual form. Intellectuals are regarded stereotypically as being "otherworldly," of having their "heads in the clouds," their "minds on higher things," and so on. The ruling class of the flying island of Laputa are intellectuals, totally absorbed with the theory of mathematics and music. They literally have their heads in the clouds and are literally cut off, in another world. Phrases like "crushed by oppression" are found in the rhetoric of politics. This is literalized by Laputa's threatening domination as it looms above Balnibarbi, its colony.

The ruling Laputians have a strange appearance: "Their Heads were all reclined either to the Right or the Left; one of their Eyes turned inward, and the other directly up to the Zenith. Their outward Garments were adorned with the Figures of Suns, Moons, and Stars, interwoven with those of Fiddles, Flutes, Harps" (III.ii.155), and other instruments. So introspective are they, that servants known as flappers have to accompany them. The flappers derive their name from the bladder and stick they carry to draw their masters' attention to the everyday world. Swift maintains an objective, descriptive tone and leaves the reader's imagination to work on the spectacle of the cock-eyed being led by a fool's bauble. At a more subtle level, Swift literalizes the idea of the mystic's inner vision: the Greek root of *mystery* means "to close the eye." The political satire presents the image of power completely cut off from its consequences, analogous to theory divorced from practice, "pure" separated from "applied" science. Swift's comedy is broad enough to accommodate both slapstick and sophistication. To a certain extent the court of Laputa hints at the contemporary court patronage of science and music in the age of Newton and Handel. The Royal Academy of Music was founded in 1719. Mathematics and music were an opportune means for Swift to carry out his satirical strategies, since both could be considered as self-subsistent worlds of proportion and number separated from the contingent world of phenomena. Members of the Royal Society had contributed papers on the geometric proportions of mathematics and music, and King George I was an avid patron of music, providing Handel with a £600 annual pension. But the satire runs deeper. Aristocratic absolutism not only cuts itself off from the executive but insulates itself from reality through an intervening mystique, taking such forms as chivalric ceremony, court theater, or various Royalist cults, like that of the "sun king" in the court of Louis XIV. Swift reverses the self-glorification of cosmic kingship in the Laputian's fear of being subject to the destructive power of the sun.

With great inventive dexterity, Swift makes Newtonian analysis of planetary motion and contemporary speculation about sunspots the daily worry of the Laputians. "For Instance; that the Earth by the continual Approaches of the Sun towards it, must in Course of time be absorbed or swallowed up. That the Face of the Sun will by Degrees be encrusted with its own Effluvia, and give no more Light to the World." Swift introduces the fear induced by Halley's prediction in 1705 of the return of the comet named after the astronomer, and continues, "That the Sun daily spending its Rays without any Nutriment to supply them, will at last be wholly consumed and annihilated; which must be attended with the Destruction of this Earth, and of all the Planets that receive their light from it" (III.ii.161).

Cosmic events millions of miles, and millions of years, away obsess them, while they are ignorant of their immediate political responsibilities—in every way "beneath" them—in Balnibarbi. Immediately before this passage there is an instance of Swift's allowing the proliferation of satiric barbs in part III to turn just slightly on himself. Many leading mathematicians in Swift's time were Whigs, and as such engaged vociferously in political debate. The analogy of the flying island, however, had exploited the idea of the intellectual remoteness of mathematicians and musicians in the Laputian, mandarin-like ruling class. Yet, presumably satirizing Newton, Gulliver records, "But, what I chiefly admired, and thought altogether unaccountable, was the strong Disposition I observed in them towards News and Politicks; perpetually enquiring into publick Affairs, giving their Judgments in

Matters of State; and passionately disputing every Inch of a Party Opinion. I have indeed observed the same Disposition among most of the Mathematicians I have known in Europe" (III.ii.160). Sensing the inconsistency but unwilling to give up an opportunist moment, Swift tries unsuccessfully to wriggle out of it: "I rather take this Quality to spring from a very common Infirmity of human Nature, inclining us to be more curious and conceited in Matters where we have least Concern" (III.ii.160–61). Since these Laputians never descend to see political reality, presumably their debates are all at a purely theoretical level. The eighteenth century took the satirical "mixed dish" a step further and delighted in the literary "olla podrida," as it was called, after the Spanish dish of incongruous ingredients. Perhaps that is how we should regard part III of *Gulliver's Travels*.

The movement of Laputa is determined by a giant loadstone, or magnet. Forces of attraction and repulsion are activated by the magnet's movement, pulling and pushing the island in an up-and-down, zig-zag path over Balnibarbi. The Tudor scientist William Gilbert became the founding father of the study of magnetism in his *De Magnete* of 1600, and the Royal Society proudly developed his work. "The central devise of the Floating Island, the 'prodigious loadstone,' is a magnification and adaptation of Gilbert's dipping-needle. Each is simply a loadstone capable of rotating vertically about a horizontal axis" (Nicolson and Mohler, 413). At the same time as he makes witty play with contemporary science, Swift applies one of the most striking metaphors in his writing—colonialist exploitation and oppression as "crushing." The genius of the satire nevertheless retains a suggestive subtlety. For example, consider the note, "this island cannot move beyond the Extent of the dominions below" (III.iii.166). Just as Swift correctly guessed at the two satellites of Mars, not discovered until 1877 (III.iii.168), this seems a prescient glimpse into the legacy of postcolonialism, in which the colony holds sway over the colonialist as much as the colonialist does over the colony. Swift's imagination thrives on the satirical analogies that may be drawn from the laws of science. Reciprocity and interdependence in magnetic fields provided a perfect emblem of colonialism. The astronomers responsible for directing the flying island's movement, when not thus engaged, spend all their time observing heavenly bodies and cataloguing, "ten thousand fixed stars" (III.iii.168): a paradigm of the divorce between theoretical science and political morality, which has increased in urgency since Swift's time.

The capital of Balnibarbi, Lagado, is usually taken to be London, while the second city, Lindalino, is interpreted as Dublin. Balnibarbi itself appears to be a composite of English and Irish social and political conditions. The sympathetic Lord Munodi, who befriends Gulliver on Balnibarbi, is sometimes identified with Lord Middleton, Lord Chancellor of Ireland, an opponent of "Wood's halfpence." The impoverished landscape of the countryside draws on Swift's own observations on the condition of Ireland. Swift may have known of Francesco Lana's *Podromo* (1670), which foresaw that technological achievement in aeronautics could be followed by aircraft used for warfare and invasion of foreign lands, with the bombing of whole cities. The politics of oppression take three forms. First, Laputa can hover over any town, depriving it of rain and sunlight; second, it can bombard the town with rocks; and third, it can descend and thereby crush life and property. But the last expedient is paradoxical. Such a descent could break the adamantine base of Laputa and bring destruction of crown and colony. The allegory is open-ended—does the master need the slave more than the slave needs the master? If Ireland were completely destroyed, how would absentee landlords get their rents? If there is no produce, is there then nothing to exploit? It was at this point that Swift wrote the account of the insurrection of Lindalino.

Readers should check that their editions contain this account in the last two pages of chapter III (III.iii.170–71). Charles Ford, "*a very worthy Gentleman,*" as he is referred to in the "Advertisement" (xxxiv), included the account of the insurrection with his manuscript additions to the first edition of *Gulliver's Travels,* which is now in the Victoria and Albert Museum, London. Ford was a friend of Swift in Ireland and presumably had access to the original manuscript. Motte must have been too alarmed at the possible sedition, and Faulkner likewise, assuming he had access to it in Dublin. The Lindalino passage was published for the first time in 1896. The episode is of great importance, as it makes explicit what is implicit throughout the voyage to

Laputa: England and Ireland

Laputa; it needs to be placed not just in the context of *Gulliver's Travels* but in the context of Swift's Irish writings.

A brief thumbnail sketch of Swift and Ireland will indicate the background.[2] The Irish Parliament could not convene without the permission of the English king and his Privy Council. In the second half of the seventeenth century, economic legislation carried out mercantilist theory: three-quarters of Irish trade was destroyed by strictly limiting Irish exports to England; this collapsed the native wool industry. Conversely, Ireland was not allowed to tax English imports. Politically, Catholics were barred from any position in administration or law; Catholic trade and ownership were controlled; primogeniture in Catholic families was forbidden, thereby breaking up inherited wealth. A range of measures ensured that the Catholic Irish were economically, politically, legally, and socially penalized for their religion. Sounding very much like the King of Brobdingnag, Edmund Burke described such procedures as "a machine of wise and elaborate contrivance; and as well fitted for the oppression, impoverishment, and degradation of a people, and the debasement, in them, of human nature itself, as ever proceeded from the perverted ingenuity of man" (Ferguson, 17).

In the distinct political grouping of Ireland, the indigenous Catholic Irish constituted the "native interest." At the other extreme, within the Dublin Pale, the "English interest," the English and Anglo-Irish supporters of English policies. In the middle was the "Irish interest," to which Swift belonged. The "Irish interest" consisted of mostly Anglo-Irish descendants of nearly two centuries who acknowledged the sovereignty of the English crown but not the sovereignty of the English Parliament. Their spokesman was William Molyneaux in *The Case of Ireland* (1698).

Political and religious affiliation largely determined Swift's sympathies. Throughout his career he resisted any proposal to repeal Test Acts designed to keep the Ulster Presbyterians out of power in Ireland. "Liberty" in Swift's writings—and epitaph—should not be confused with its modern-day democratic and egalitarian meaning. Swift inherited a worldview that was still generally hierarchical when it came to social class and rulership. "Liberty" was Old Whig liberty from absolutist tyranny, not universal suffrage. The mob, the *vulgus mobile*, or fickle crowd, was anarchic and dangerous. What enlarged Swift's empathy was the economics of human suffering. In the court of St. James aristocratic heads listened to the latest Handel, on Laputa ears were attuned to the music of the spheres, while below in the Irish mud was heard the wail of death from starvation.

From one point of view, the Gaelic Irish were papists and therefore politically dangerous. But seen as people, their degradation and suffering inflicted by the economic measures of England made them objects of compassion. Swift identified "Irish interest" as national interest, which worked up to a point, since no one else was going to help the peasantry.

In 1720 the English government passed the Declaratory Act to tighten the screws on Ireland and make it even more dependent. Swift responded in the *Proposal for the Universal Use of Irish Manufacture* (1720) by arguing that the Irish could fight back by refusing to buy English goods and instead rely on their own manufacture, the economic principle of domestic consumption of domestic products. Then the affair of "Wood's halfpence" arose as Swift was engaged with part III of *Gulliver's Travels*. The Lindalino episode is a final shot in what was to be a pyrrhic victory. "About three years before my Arrival among them" (III.iii.170), Gulliver begins—that is, approximately 1722, when rumors of Walpole's plan for a copper coinage had spread throughout Ireland. A deficiency was to be met by granting a patent to William Wood, an iron dealer, to coin £100,800 worth of copper halfpennies. Objections were that such an amount was wildly excessive— Ireland's total currency was £400,000. The copper content was too low, and according to Gresham's law bad money would drive out good. Minting at Bristol, instead of London, would be beyond proper supervision, thus counterfeiting would be easier.

In 1724, Swift entered the fray in the persona of a humble Dublin draper, or drapier, and began the sequence known as *The Drapier's Letters*. Presumably because of their detailed polemical topicality, these are the least read of Swift's satires, which is regrettable, since they contain some of his most pungent and combative writing. In the Lindalino episode the citizens revolt, seize the governor, and erect four towers, topped by magnets, "to burst therewith the adamantine

Bottom of the Island" (III.iii.170). An additional weapon is "a vast Quantity of the most combustible Fewel" (III.iii.170), a possible allusion to *The Drapier's Letters*. "It was eight Months before the King had perfect Notice that the Lindalinians were in Rebellion" (III.iii.170). This Laputian remoteness probably refers to the eight-month delay between the appearance of an anti-Wood tract and the king's recalling the lord lieutenant of Ireland, the Duke of Grafton, to London to explain the situation.

Of the seven *Drapier's Letters*, five appeared in 1724. The Drapier mask, or persona, brought home to the Irish middle classes the reality of economic exploitation and catastrophe. Unfortunately for Walpole and Wood, a constitutional safeguard meant that only gold and silver were compulsory legal tender. The Drapier seized on this legality—no one could force the Irish to accept the copper coins—and emphasized the practical difficulty of weight and carriage in his wildly exaggerated calculations for daily use. In his second letter, the Drapier challenged Wood's promise that no one should receive more than 5 pence as amounting to high treason, since it assumed a prerogative not even allowed to the king. As the situation continued, Swift's attack widened to the political power that made Wood's halfpence possible. In Cork a shipment of coin was prevented from coming ashore, and the vessel was threatened with burning. Swift's fourth letter moves from opposition to sedition as the Drapier calls into question the validity of Ireland's legislative dependence. A reward of £300 was offered for the identity of the writer whom everybody knew, but nobody would betray. The authorities wanted the Drapier behind the walls of Dublin castle, but Swift remained behind his satiric mask. With great bravura Swift apologizes in the next letter, since all his views were taken from the political philosophers whose ideas provided a foundation for the Whig revolution upheld by the London ministerial Whigs in pursuit of the Drapier. The sixth letter in Swift's own voice, was withheld, but the seventh spelled out the logical conclusion the Drapier had been working toward—William Wood symbolized *all* of England's exploitation. Satire succeeded. The patent was withdrawn, but the condition of Ireland remained.

In the Lindalino rebellion, Laputa hovers threateningly over the city while the citizens demand "Redress of all their Grievances"

(III.iii.190). The king is provoked into his second and third strategy. Lindalino is bombarded, then the flying island descends to crush its victims, but the controllers find that the speed is dangerously uncontrollable. The "Officers of the Loadstone" conduct an experiment, and an allegory of Wood's halfpence follows. Small pieces of adamant, like that of the island's foundation, compounded with "Iron mineral" (III.iii.171), are lowered on a line. The effect is so violent that the king desists from further descent of Laputa, which would bring about its destruction.

Ireland's boycott had achieved its immediate end, but none of the fundamental political and economic problems had been resolved. A bad harvest in 1727 brought famine. In a nonsatirical economic pamphlet written that year, *A Short View of the State of Ireland,* Swift spelled out a positive economic program by examining the causes and effects of prosperity. In an undated sermon, "Causes of the Wretched Condition of Ireland," Swift had particularly bemoaned the effect of absentee landlords draining capital from Ireland. No image could be more "absent," in every sense, than that of the Laputians. The *Short View* provides a pungent contrast with *A Modest Proposal.* In straightforward, summary prose, Swift itemizes the necessary factors for a nation's economic welfare and the situation in Ireland. The country has good soil and climate, but the peasantry is not encouraged to take advantage of it. Ireland has many natural ports suitable for trade, but they are not used. Next to none of the timber cut down in the country has been used for shipping or housing. Exports are prohibited. Ireland cannot make its own laws. The land is not properly maintained, and the countryside is depopulated by turning over the fields from arable to pasture. Not only are landlords absent but so is the ruler, whether king or viceroy. There are no visitors to bring in wealth. Most members of the population are debarred from any office. Both luxury goods for the few, and essentials for the many, are all imported from England. Paradoxically, the "evidence" found by those for Ireland's prosperity demonstrates the reverse: rack-renting is a sign of desperation, not wealth; interest is low because there are no borrowers, as there is no trade; land is expensive because there is nothing else to buy; tenants increase prices of goods to pay the high rent; workmen employ each other on buildings nobody can afford; bankers thrive by selling Ireland's stock of silver and gold abroad.

With such paradox in reality, perhaps the ironies of *A Modest Proposal* seem a little less bizarre? Swift's great pamphlet of 1729 transposes the economic program implied in the *Short View* to satire, which, along with the oppression of the flying island, provides Swift with his most forceful literalization of the metaphorical. With the cold stultification of rage, Swift tells his readers to eat the children, as everything else has been "devoured" by exploitation. We recoil in horror from the truth of the most savage irony in English satire: a quick death in barbaric cannibalism is more humane than protracted suffering and a painful end—the inevitable reality while conditions remained unchanged in Ireland.

8

Balnibarbi and Glubbdubdrib:
Ancients and Moderns

Ever curious, and neglected by the abstract Laputians, Gulliver wishes to visit Balnibarbi and its capital, Lagado. Lord Munodi, held in contempt for his limitations in music, is to be his host. Unlike the Laputian monarch, Munodi has a humanist sense of curiosity and "desired to be informed in the Affairs of *Europe,* the Laws and Customs, the Manners and Learning of the several Countries where I had travelled" (III.iv.173). Munodi embodies the traditional positives of the class and culture of an inherited patrician aristocracy and landed gentry. Resistant to "Innovation" and content to follow the "old Forms" (III.iv.176), negotiating between court, country, and countryside, Munodi combines Horatian retirement with Ciceronian public duty. From an allegorical point of view, he represents the best of Old Whig and Tory ideals rendered anachronistic in the 1720s. In a word, Munodi is an ancient.

When Gulliver is shown Lagado and the surrounding country-side, it is immediately obvious from the Irish tracts discussed in the preceding chapter that Swift is drawing on his experience of Dublin and its environs: "the Houses . . . most of them out of Repair. The

People . . . Eyes fixed . . . generally in Rags . . . neither did I observe any Expectation either of Corn or Grass, although the Soil appeared to be excellent" (III.iv.174). In contrast, Munodi's townhouse and country estate are well ordered and cultivated in the midst of barren waste. When Gulliver describes the country house, and the noble lord explains the contempt in which he is held, in one paragraph we find the two key terms for this chapter—ancient and modern. "We came at length to the House, which was indeed a noble Structure, built according to the best Rules of ancient Architecture," Gulliver records. Munodi laments that he is under pressure to pull down his houses and destroy his agriculture, replacing both "as modern Usage required" (III.iv.175). False magnificence as an abuse of classical architecture in the Palladian revival was satirized by Pope in the "Epistle of Burlington." *Gulliver's Travels* is recalled in the lines on the chilly expanses of Timon's villa, "Greatness, with Timon, dwells in such a draught / As brings all Brobdingnag before your thought" (ll.103–4).

Lord Munodi explains that the academy of projectors in Lagado had been founded after an inspired visit to Laputa by virtuosi intent on experimental innovation in every sphere of life—building, agriculture, and manufacture. The combination of untried technology and speculative theory had proved wholly destructive, since nothing was ever completed. As an example he cites the situation he was forced into when persuaded to abandon his perfectly satisfactory water mill in favor of one built halfway up a mountain, which therefore needed water to be driven uphill, before it could be worked. Swift thus satirizes contemporary experiment in hydraulics, which seemed nonsensical in practice. He was not to know that aqueducts would eventually be regarded as one of the great achievements of industrial technology and architecture.

The academy of projectors represents Swift's most concerted attack on a major branch of modernism—the rise of experimental science, symbolized by the foundation of the Royal Society. Swift's earliest great satire, *A Tale of a Tub,* and an appendage to it, though an independent work, *The Battle of the Books* (1704), had been wholly concerned with the idea of modernism. From one point of view *Gulliver's Travels* is part of this critique, since Gulliver embodies many aspects of early-eighteenth-century modernity. The subject is a huge one, both in Swift's writing and as an issue in the development of Western culture, particularly since the Renaissance. Hence the specific focus applied here to Balnibarbi and Glubbdubdrib.

The two targets of modernism in *A Tale of a Tub* are the corruptions in religion and in learning brought about by the moderns. The religious moderns are those of a dissenting background, like Gulliver, whose "enthusiasm"—a key term for Swift and his age, meaning fanaticism—threatened both the established church and the state. The gamut of nonconformity went all the way from Anabaptists to Atheists. The moderns corrupting learning were at one extreme Grub Street hacks, as Swift considered Defoe. (The London street gave its name to those journalistic mercenaries who wrote anything for cash.) At the other extreme were those classical scholars attempting to establish texts on a scientific philological basis, represented by Dr. Richard Bentley. For Swift, modernism exhibited the sin of pride, an arrogance that took the form of spiritual and intellectual autonomy divorced from any dependency on religious or humanistic tradition. Like the experimental scientists, the moderns of religion and learning were empirical, drawing only on the source of firsthand experience of the Spirit or the Text. For conservatives like Swift, the truths of human experiences were mediated by history embodied in the authority of hierarchic institutions of Church and Society. They did not derive from aberrant subjectivity or self-sufficient individualism.

In *The Battle of the Books* a mock-heroic fight takes place between representatives of ancient and modern learning. In the field of science and philosophy, Plato and Aristotle are ranged against Descartes and Bacon; Galen and Hippocrates against Paracelsus and William Harvey. For the academy of Lagado and the Royal Society, Francis Bacon is the crucial figure. Bacon was the father of experimental science and the idea of a cooperative community of natural philosophers, as scientists were generally known in the seventeenth century. Solomon's House as a seat of learning for the new science, sponsored by government, had seemed a utopian dream in Bacon's *New Atlantis* (1627), but with hindsight it is now acknowledged as an imaginative forerunner of the Royal Society. Bacon's scientific method was empirical, using observation and experiment as a basis for gathering data, thereby providing the factual basis for an inductive approach. Induction works from effects (observable things) to causes, not the other way round, as in Aristotle. The Aristotelian deductive method considers anything as following from a given hypothesis, that is, working from an assumed cause in a given explanatory formula. Bacon was concerned with materials and things; he was utilitarian and practical. In contrast, Aristotle seemed speculative, concerned with ideas and the words for ideas, separate from things in the world of experience. Thomas Hobbes led the moderns' attack on Aristotelian scientific method and dismissed all the Aristotelian terminology—being and not being, substance and accidents, form and matter, potentiality and actuality, substratum, privation, etc.—as empty words. The new science was to be experimental, skeptical, and open-ended, not stultified by precept, axiom, and dogma.[1]

The anti-scholastic philosophy of nominalism distrusted Aristotelian logic, believing that reality lay in things, not in syllogisms. This skepticism influenced early scientists like Bacon and followers in the Royal Society who wished to purge language of rhetoric and pseudoscientific obfuscation. Swift seizes on this for ready-made satire in the academy of Lagado. "An Expedient was therefore offered, that since Words are only Names for *Things,* it would be more convenient for all Men to carry about them, such *Things* as were necessary to express the particular Business they are to discourse on" (III.v.184). Applying a logic of absurdity, Swift literalizes the philosophical premise by having the virtuosi "adhere to the new Scheme of expressing themselves by *Things;* which hath only this Inconvenience attending it; that if a Man's Business be very great, and of various Kinds, he must be obliged in Proportion to carry a greater Bundle of *Things* upon his Back, unless he can afford one or two strong Servants to attend him" (III.v.185). Thomas Sprat's official *History of the Royal Society* (1667) emphasized the necessity of rejecting "all the amplifications, digressions and swellings of style: to return back to the primitive purity, and shortness, when men deliver'd so many things, almost in an equal number of *words.*"

Between Bacon and the foundation of the Royal Society was what was known as the Invisible College, a group of scientists who met at

Oxford in the 1640s. At the Restoration, the Invisible College met in London at Gresham College, and after a lecture in 1660, by Sir Christopher Wren, proposals were made for the foundation of a society, which eventually received a royal charter in 1662. Following Bacon's fundamental principle, the Royal Society was to collect data on a wide range of subjects, covering the heavens and the earth, animals and nature, human being and society: "The scope of the Society's inquiries may be gathered from the names of the committees and their purposes. Among these were the mathematical, the astronomical and optical, the chemical, the agricultural, and those for correspondence and the history of trade. The communications were classified into the following, among other categories: mechanics and trade; journals of the weather; statics and hydraulics; architecture, ship-building, geography, navigation, voyages, and travels; pharmacy and chemistry; monsters and longevity; grammar, chronology, history and antiquities."[2]

The work of the Royal Society was published as the *Philosophical Transactions.* Science was popular and these were widely read, eventually in abridgements and in a three-volume edition of selected papers, published in 1705 as *Miscellanea Curiosa.* The discoveries and redirections taken by experimental science inevitably led to comparisons between the ancients and the moderns, to the former's resounding disadvantage. Arguably the most famous laudatory work championing the moderns was Joseph Glanvil's *Plus Ultra* (1668). Modern superiority in chemistry, anatomy, mathematics, and all branches of science is celebrated with particular reference to such glories of modernism as printing and the compass, telescope, microscope, and thermometer. The particular pride of Englishmen was the discovery of the circulation of the blood by their countryman, William Harvey.

At the end of the century, the substance of Glanvil's book was adapted and expanded by William Wotton to include the superiority of the moderns in all spheres of learning, including the arts, in *Reflections upon Ancient and Modern Learning* (1694). Wotton's book was part of a controversy begun by Swift's early patron, Sir William Temple, which occasioned a number of volumes over several years culminating in *The Battle of the Books,* which satirized the whole issue in mock-heroic terms. In brief, the English battle of ancients versus moderns began with

Balnibarbi and Glubbdubdrib: Ancients and Moderns

Temple's essay "Upon Ancient and Modern Learning," which had censured two late-seventeenth-century works praising modern learning and poetry over that of the ancient world. Unfortunately, Temple chose as examples of the superiority of ancient prose the fables of Aesop and the epistles of Phalaris. Both works were proved to be forgeries, Dr. Richard Bentley producing a massive folio, *Dissertation upon the Epistles of Phalaris* (1699), as evidence. Swift's satire brings comic relief to what can seem a tediously pedantic affair (though wholly characteristic of the period), but Wotton's book remains as a major document in British and European cultural history, with considerable intellectual range, not just polemical topicality. The wider sociological issues will be raised along with the spirits on Glubbdubdrib. In the academy of Lagado Swift chose to develop considerably the satiric asides on modern science in *The Battle of the Books*.

In earlier criticism it used to be said that Swift was ignorant of contemporary science. He may have been unsympathetic and uncomprehending, but the research of Marjorie Nicolson and Nora M. Mohler shows quite clearly that Swift, like many others, studied quite closely the *Philosophical Transactions* and the *Miscellanea Curiosa*.[3] The satire on projectors and experiments may well have literary allusions to predecessors like Rabelais, but in nearly every case Swift derived his seeming satirical fantasy from the recorded accounts of experiments he had studied.

It is on record that Swift actually visited the Royal Society. As he wrote to Stella on 13 December 1710, "then to Bedlam; then dined at the Chophouse behind the Exchange; then to Gresham College (but the keeper was not at home), and concluded the night at the puppet-show."[4] For the social historian of a structuralist persuasion there are materials here for a whole volume; the significance of Bedlam will be returned to in the last chapter of this study, but we must now visit the grand academy of Lagado with Gulliver.

The first project Gulliver encounters is among the most celebrated for its satire. An unkempt, dirty figure "had been Eight Years upon a Project for extracting Sub-Beams out of Cucumbers, which were to be put into Vials hermetically sealed, and let out to warm the air in raw inclement Summers" (III.v.178). Experiments on plant and animal respiration had shown how certain fruits and vegetables (apples particularly, but not cucumbers) generated great quantities of air. What today is understood as photosynthesis is indebted to experiments reported to the Royal Society by John Hales concerning the effect of the sun's light and heat on the earth and on plants' absorption and "respiration." Swift's satire works by a linguistic short circuit of a botanic process, cleverly introducing an accurate term for sealing glass tubes, but also a term associated with the mumbo-jumbo of seventeenth-century occultism—"hermetic."

Remarkably, "There was a Man born blind, who had several Apprentices in his own Condition: Their Employment was to mix Colours for Painters, which their Master taught them to distinguish by feeling and smelling" (III.v.179). The case of a real blind man from Maastricht had been reported to Robert Boyle and recorded in his *Philosophical Works* (1725). Perhaps best known for *The Sceptical Chymist* (1661), and probably the most versatile scientist of the day, Robert Boyle was an archmodern. It was he who in studying elements and compounds repudiated the utility of Aristotle's categories of matter into earth, air, fire, and water. Though the blind Dutchman believed he identified colors by touch, Boyle suspected that the different dyes for various colors had different smells. Swift astutely picks up the point, which indicates either that he had read Boyle or that the paradoxical nature of the case had made it an item of coffeehouse discussion.

Gulliver proceeds to another projector, who is attempting to develop a substitute for the silkworm by feeding spiders highly colored flies to get them to spin colored thread. Swift crossed two papers from the *Philosophical Transactions*. A Monsieur Bon had recommended the silk of short-legged spiders, and elsewhere a correspondent reported on dyes like cochineal, derived from insects. In such a bizarre situation Gulliver feels a little queasy and is directed to a specialist in colic who experiments on dogs by means of bellows inserted in the anus to admit or withdraw air. An experiment in artificial respiration on a dog is recorded in the *Transactions,* but Swift simply makes a Rabelaisian choice of another orifice. Satire often draws on scatology, but even here there was a scientific precedent in a speculative paper on the possibility of reversing bowel peristalsis by an artificially induced anti-peristaltic motion, to evacuate by the mouth.

The projector trying to reduce human excrement to its original constituents seemingly has no scientific origin but refers to a comparable situation in Rabelais. This revolting image perhaps brings home the humanist ancients' contempt for the modern projector. To survey past history from the position of the 1720s, asking what presents the summation of human achievement—though Newton's discovery of the laws of gravity was revered—it must have been hard to see what the examination of spittle under the microscope had to offer against Homer's *Iliad* or Virgil's *Aeneid*. But with the fuller perspectives allowed the contemporary world when surveying the history of technology, it is striking how some of the very things made ludicrous in Swift's satire have been realized in the twentieth century. Human excrement has not been reduced to its original constituents, but, analogously, for many years farmers have processed cattle slurry into methane, a useful fuel. Spinach has been used to create electricity. Quoted here is a much-used seminar item, originally reported in the *Guardian* newspaper in the mid-1970s: "Japanese researchers claim to have found a way of using spinach to convert the sun's rays into commercial electricity. Ultra-pure chlorophyll extracted from spinach and other green vegetables is refined into a film which, when exposed to the sun, generates electrical power." One projector hopes to breed wool-less sheep (III.v.182). Given the rise of cheap manufactured fibers in recent decades, many sheep breeders have sought means of raising fatter animals for their meat and actually reducing the fleece.

One of the original illustrations of *Gulliver's Travels* shows an experimental word-processing machine (III.v.181). Swift guessed at the two satellites of Mars, and this machine satirizing "speculative learning" appears to have anticipated the revolution that has come to shape the lives of most people on earth—information retrieval systems, culminating in the ever-developing sophistication of computer technology, by which, in fact, this book was produced. Perhaps a resonant local irony may be pointed out. An architect-projector experiments on building from the roof down (III.v.179). Since the 1960s huge power-jacks have been used to build downward from the top story, and this is precisely how the Bank of Ireland was constructed in Dublin.

It was noted above that the economies of subsistence and starvation exacerbated Swift's imagination, compassion, and satire. The King of Brobdingnag reflects this when he tells Gulliver "that whoever could make two Ears of Corn, or two Blades of Grass to grow upon a Spot of Ground where only one grew before; would deserve better for Mankind, and do more essential Service to his Country, than the whole Race of Politicians put together" (II.vii.130). Swift was unable to grasp that the way to achieve this is by the experiments of what today is called soil science. The Royal Society anticipated this, and one of its early panels was a "Georgicall Committee," set up in 1664, which, by means of correspondents, carried out a detailed survey of English agriculture. In fact, it was in this period that Robert Boyle recognized the efficacy of chemical fertilizers, knowledge that derived from the rejection of Aristotle and the establishment of chemistry on a modern scientific footing.

Gulliver visited the academy as an enthusiastic modern, but Swift's satire here is aimed directly at what the mariner sees rather than at his character—irony is generated by the various situations rather than by psychology. In chapter VI, in the account of the school of political projectors, Gulliver takes on a rhetorical function found on Brobdingnag. With the experimental projectors the real is made lunatic and taken seriously. At the outset with the political projectors, the serious is taken as unreal lunacy. The satiric sleight of hand Swift uses is to confound the distinction between learning and lunacy, the Royal Society and Bedlam, as if after visiting both, as we have seen, they reappeared together in the phantasmagoria of a dream.

Juxtaposition and contrast give considerable power to the shock tactic as the reader is taken completely unawares. In the first line Gulliver remarks that the professors appear "wholly out of their Senses" (III.vi.187). The account of some fantastic utopia is anticipated, but such recommendations are made as "of persuading Monarchs to chuse Favourites upon the Score of their Wisdom, Capacity and Virtue; of teaching Ministers to consult the publick Good; of rewarding Merit, great Abilities and eminent Services." All these, to Gulliver, are "wild impossible Chimaeras, that never entered before into the Heart of Man to conceive" (III.vi.187). Some of the wittiest, most inventive, and cutting satire on politicians then (and now) follows, in what should be placed along with the most mordant pieces in Swift's writing. In one section we find an inadvertent image for the dialectical mode throughout *Gulliver's Travels.* Where parties are violently opposed, it is recommended that the leaders' heads be cut in half and exchanged: "the two half Brains being left to debate the Matter between themselves with the Space of one Scull, would soon come to a good Understanding" (III.vi.189). Ironically, the critics are still debating the relationship between Gulliver's brain and Swift's brain, but it is hoped that a dialectical approach will work toward an "Understanding."

Rather than delay a month waiting in the port of Maldonada for a ship to Luggnagg, Gulliver decides to visit Glubbdubdrib, the Island of Sorcerers, or Magicians. The island is so called because of the governor's ability to call up ghosts from the dead. Dialogues with the dead and/or descents into the underworld are part of the Lucianic mode. On Glubbdubdrib the conjured spirits speak only the truth, "for Lying was a Talent of no Use in the lower World" (III.vii.195). Gulliver mostly views representatives of different classes of people in ancient and modern history, including politicians, nobles, soldiers, and patriots. In addition, recalling *The Battle of the Books,* figures from ancient and modern learning come into view, the moderns somewhat embarrassed by their illustrious predecessors.

The context of Swift's *Battle* is much more significant than that of a young writer wittily defending the cause of his patron. Sir William Temple had taken exception to Fontenelle's *Digression on the Ancients and Moderns* (1688), which had praised the poetry at the court of Louis XIV as superior to that of Virgil and Horace under Augustus. Intermittently, in the course of Western history, civilizations have either bemoaned their sense of inferiority or applauded their sense of superiority when looking back on the achievements of Greece and Rome. Such concerns inevitably played their part in the development of Renaissance humanism. Though it is perhaps easy to dismiss the sycophantic gestures within a despotic court, the underlying issues are deeper than a question of aesthetic preferences. In fifteenth-century Florence, moderns championed the triumph of the Italian vernacular over contemporary neoclassicizing humanist worship of Ciceronian Latin.[5] In his praise of Michelangelo, Vasari believed that the artist had outdone ancients, moderns, and even nature itself.

In England, France, and Italy, the recognition of the accomplishments of contemporary science and literature depended to a large extent on how history was understood. This understanding was not a neutral scholarly or intellectual activity but the result of a prior condition, the belief in history as progressive and ameliorative or as declining and degenerative. All of these ideas are part of an ideological network that is fundamentally political. In the breakdown of social and intellectual structures that constituted the Renaissance and Reformation there emerged a new middle class, together with nationalism, coinciding with scientific and artistic achievement: Shakespeare and Bacon, Milton and Newton. The past could be respected but need not necessarily be revered as in the present of English nationhood incomparable modern figures had appeared. The dominant image of the ancients versus the moderns is that of the giant and the pygmy. The ancients are giants, it was claimed, and the moderns pygmies. But then it was said that the modern pygmy is able to stand on a giant's shoulders and see farther than he. Temple replied that the modern pygmy was shortsighted, whereas Bacon turned the whole thing round by claiming that the so-called moderns were really the ancients, as the world had grown that much older since the period of a Homer or Virgil. Thus the true ancients, Bacon and his contemporaries, were in receipt of so much more knowledge that, of necessity, they were bound to be superior and, by implication, giants in their own right. Temple and Swift tended to reduce this issue to the moral question of the pride and arrogance of the moderns, in Temple's word, their "sufficiency." For Temple, the moderns were overreachers, going beyond what is ordained spiritually and intellectually by God. This theological implication may be reexamined in political terms as reactionary conservatism.

In contrast, Wotton's ideological basis in his *Reflections* is the precise opposite—a progressive relativism. Wotton sees culture as the product of political and social conditions, not as the result of unique personal genius. Thus, in the right circumstances, a British orator as great as the greatest Athenian orator, Demosthenes, could appear. Historiography as a branch of ideology can be seen in the circular notion of history that went hand in hand with the seemingly observable fact of *translatio imperii,* or "translation of empire." History showed that the seat of empire went from the Greeks to the Romans to the Holy Roman Empire of the Germans. It was considered that a parallel "translation" of arts and learning took place as well: Charlemagne's court, the twelfth-century Renaissance, and Renaissance courts fondly claiming to be recipients of such progress, which reinforced nationalist assertion. The rivalry between Henry VIII and Frances I is a good example. The pageantry of the Field of Cloth of Gold held near Calais in 1520 was intended not only to exhibit the chivalric prowess of England and France but also to promote the competing credentials of each as the foremost embodiment of Renaissance courtliness and culture in the eyes of Europe.

In Godfrey Goodman's *The Fall of Man* (1616) and George Hakewill's *Apologie* (1627), two ideas of history are opposed. Goodman adopts the physiological model—history is like a life: birth, maturity, and then decay. Hakewill adopts the notion of natural cycles and the idea of "reflourishing," paralleling the familiar idea of Renaissance, or rebirth. For optimistic historians of the eighteenth century, particularly the French Physiocrats, history showed an ever-increasing progression in human betterment. Linear decline is downhill, progress was a linear march to the summits of secular perfectibility. Swift's historicism in relation to ancients versus moderns, in spite of his vestigial revolutionary Whiggism, is made apparent on Glubbdubdrib with the all-pervasive sense of degeneration—physical, moral, social, political, and spiritual.

Since many of the value judgments are made not just by the spirits but by Gulliver himself, we see that he has become a spokesman for the ancients, often echoing Swift's beliefs—above all in the brief but memorable encounter with the sextumvirate. Discussion here will not be sequential, but according to the groups mentioned above, beginning with literature, philosophy, and science.

In *The Battle of the Books* Homer confronts Sir William Davenant, royalist author of *Gondibert: An Heroick Poem* (1651). This substantial poem was preceded by Davenant's substantial preface to Thomas Hobbes, and Hobbes's reply. Such fulsome preliminaries as a characteristic of early publishing culminate in Dryden's multiple dedications and prefaces to his translation of Virgil, which infuriated Swift and contributed considerably to the opening design of *A Tale of a Tub.* On Glubbdubdrib, Swift satirizes an aspect of scholarly publishing he considered to be archmodernism—the tradition of comment, which print had facilitated, ultimately sinking the text in a quagmire of annotation. Homer appears with his commentators, who, out of a sense of shame, normally keep their distance in the lower world. Gulliver presents Petrus Ramus and Duns Scotus to Aristotle. Ramus had undertaken an influential Renaissance revision of Aristotelian logic and rhetoric, while the medieval schoolman, now only remembered for the word *Dunce,* had written a commentary on Aristotle. Mention of the schoolmen reminds us that St. Thomas Aquinas had accomplished one of the most momentous cultural syntheses of history by combining Aristotelian philosophy with Christian faith, the final cause with Divine purpose. Another philosopher who many would say had achieved the reverse was Descartes.

Aristotle had defeated Descartes in *The Battle of the Books,* and now he confronts him again, but in a more peaceful manner. Aristotle apologizes for the shortcomings of his science and predicts that the vorticism of Descartes (the rotary movement of atoms), the epicurean atomism of Descartes critic Pierre Gassendi (the fortuitous collision of atoms), and even the "Attraction" (III.viii.198), or gravity, of Newton will be superseded. Descartes's vortices of particles whirling about the universe are satirized humorously in *The Battle of the Books,* but classical atomism has had a long run, and Newton's laws of gravity prevailed until Einstein's general theory of relativity. Cartesian physics threw out all such notions as Aristotle's final cause and subjected phenomena to a mathematical examination of mass and motion, a mechanistic speculative philosophy quite different from the empiricism of experimental science.

Mechanistic physics separated God from his creation and had no place for Christ the Redeemer or any theological concept at all. For

the Middle Ages, Aristotle's "Unmoved Prime Mover" could be identified with God, but for Pascal, reflecting on the Copernican system and
gazing into the night sky, those infinite spaces were terrifying. Gulliver
records Aristotle's belief "that new Systems of Nature were but new
Fashions, which would vary in every Age; and even those who pretend
to demonstrate them from Mathematical Principles, would flourish but
a short Period of Time, and be out of Vogue when that was determined" (III.viii.198). There are layers of irony here, since the subsequent development of science has indeed demonstrated this, but such
surprising liberalism is quite at odds with the fierce dogmatic insistence
on Aristotle's authority in the universities and among the ancients.
However we appraise Swift's ideological position, subsequent history
has indeed shown that science and secularism go hand in hand. But
decline of another sort appears in the further contrasts of ancient and
modern, which contribute to Gulliver's growing disillusionment.

The ancient world is not uniformly praised by Gulliver, whereas
the modern seems almost wholly contemptible, but for the figure of Sir
Thomas More. Ancient myths are briefly debunked; Alexander died of
drink, not poisoning; Hannibal denies the story about breaking alpine
rocks with fire and vinegar. Echoing the Old Whig ideals of 1689,
Gulliver recounts, "I chiefly fed mine Eyes with beholding the
Destroyers of Tyrants and Usurpers, and the Restorers of Liberty to
oppressed and injured Nations" (III.vii.196). Chief of these is Marcus
Brutus, upholder of republican liberty against Julius Caesar, who
reveals to Gulliver that "his Ancestor *Junius, Socrates, Epaminondas,
Cato* the Younger, Sir *Thomas More* and himself, were perpetually
together: A *Sextumvirate* to which all the Ages of the World cannot
add a Seventh" (III.vii.196).[6] Though Swift abhorred the execution of
Charles I, he was influenced by the writings of Algernon Sidney, who
was put to death for his anti-monarchical, republican politics in 1683.
While believing in a limited monarchy and balanced constitution, Swift
could admire republicans of antiquity for their resistance to tyranny,
largely symbolized by the sextumvirate with its one honorific modern,
Sir Thomas More.

To Gulliver's vision of modern politicians, nobles, courtiers, and
those otherwise with a place in history, Swift brings into play serial
rhetoric. Swift's satire sometimes uses a logic of absurdity. The serial

technique is like a form of hyperbole, not reason, challenging the reader to redress its cumulative sense of outrage and dismay. "Modern" politicians, compared with those of the Roman senate of "Heroes and Demy-Gods," appeared "a knot of Pedlars, Pick-pockets, Highwaymen and Bullies" (III.vii.196). The progenitors of illustrious modern families turn out to be tradesmen, servants, and clergy, conferring not aristocratic blue blood but venereal disease. A passing satirical swipe raises the whole vexed question of rhetorical historiography—historians offering idealized portraits of exemplary character and action, usually of patrons, rather than unpalatable truths of corruption and criminality. To illustrate "how much the Race of human kind was degenerate among us, within these Hundred Years past," Gulliver invokes the idealized vision of the old English Yeoman who embodied for Whig historians a patriotism and liberty untainted by "every Vice and Corruption than can possible be learned at Court" (III.viii.202). The belief in degeneration is felt throughout *Gulliver's Travels*. What the King of Brobdingnag invites Gulliver to recognize after his lengthy panegyric is now realized in visionary form. Perhaps the old treatise on the degeneration of human nature owned by Glumdalclitch's governess (II.vii.131–32) was Goodman's *The Fall of Man*? At all events, the external vision on Glubbdubdrib undergoes a further internalized dimension in Houyhnhnmland.

As if in illustration of court politics of tyranny, the immediately following account of Gulliver's brief visit to the king of Luggnagg offers a vivid paradigm. Court protocol determined that visitors approach the throne crawling on their belly and licking the floor, which has been customarily sprinkled with dust. Those who spit or wipe their mouths in the king's presence are executed.

Having viewed the resurrected dead, before his return home via Japan, Gulliver meets the undead of Luggnagg, the immortal Struldbruggs. This section of the *Travels* is often glossed by commentators with reference to such contexts as reports to the Royal Society on longevity, the myth of the mortal Tithonus, who gained immortality but not eternal youth, or Juvenal's portrayal of the miseries of old age in the tenth *Satire*. But these sources themselves, as Juvenal intimates, derive from what the Spanish philosopher Miguel de Unamuno calls in the title of his most famous book *The Tragic Sense of Life* (1913). Man fears death and nothingness and yearns for immortality. Not tied to canons of realism, having all the freedom of the satirist, Swift's fantasy turns the hypothetical into the real. Dr. Johnson takes advantage of a comparable mode in his extensive parable *Rasselas* (1759). In Dr. Johnson's Happy Valley every want is fulfilled, yet satiety brings boredom, and for Rasselas, the Abyssinian prince, gratification brings dissatisfaction. "If only . . ." and "I wish that . . ." are phrases probably uttered by everyone at one time or other. The Struldbruggs of book III offer a chastening spectacle of decrepitude and a paradoxical indifference to life. For Swift and Johnson the moral is the same. Humankind's first folly is to ignore the essential, inescapable, limiting conditions of life. Both Prince Rasselas and Gulliver eventually return home, their travels completed, but with vastly different understandings of human nature.

9

Houyhnhnmland: Equine Utopia

Once more the indomitable traveler finds himself abandoned in a strange land. Lapsing in prudence, Gulliver had inadvertently recruited buccaneers who suborned the rest of the crew into piracy, marooning the captain. Yet, resourceful in adversity, Gulliver carries "some Bracelets, Glass Rings, and other Toys" to placate the indigenous "Savages" (IV.i.225) he expects to meet. Nervous of an attack by the natives, he relates, "I walked very circumspectly for fear of being surprised" (IV.i.225). Elsewhere we have seen that Swift, when he chooses, can use deliberate, heavy-handed irony. This is an example of the reverse, an ironic allusive subtlety only for the more discerning reader. Gulliver as traveler means one thing, while Swift in the same words as his persona means another.

WISDOM AND FOLLY

As narrator-character from a dissenting background, in dangerous circumstances, Gulliver echoes a text of his persuasion from St. Paul, "See then that ye walk circumspectly, not as fools, but as wise"

(Ephesians 5.15). It could be said that this is quite naturalistic and psychologically acute, Gulliver bracing himself with faith. But from the all-embracing perspective of satire the allusion is hugely comic. Swift allows the unwitting Gulliver the Swiftian technique of literalizing the metaphorical, or, in this case, the spiritual. "Walk" in St. Paul has much wider spiritual meaning than simple movement. And the second half of the verse inevitably evoked by Gulliver reminds us of the satirical relation of folly and wisdom throughout the *Travels*. Gulliver has encountered much folly and some wisdom. He himself has frequently been foolish, and just occasionally wise, as the dialectical irony shifts between voyager and satirist. Furthermore, the echo of St. Paul reminds the wary reader of the possible folly of credulity and the wisdom of skepticism; we should read circumspectly, especially when we are told the story of a land governed by rational horses.

Gulliver is not hit with a native arrow but is struck by the appearance of most peculiar animals. Swift is extremely subtle in the way in which, just before this, he introduces a suggestion: "I saw many Tracks of human Feet, and some of Cows, but most of Horses" (IV.i.225). "Human" creates an expectation (we recall Robinson Crusoe's famous discovery of the footprint), but in the description of the "animals" that follows, the word *human* is not repeated and there is no direct comparison with human beings. Neither is there a comparison with apes or monkeys. Male and female are discerned according to exposed genitals, however, and these animals often stand on their hind feet. The males are bearded like goats, and they climb trees by means of their claws with the nimbleness of squirrels. The females have lank dugs. A "fore Paw" (IV.i.226) is mentioned, but never hands. Unlike apes and monkeys, these creatures are only hairy in places. For some details, as discussed in chapter 1, Swift draws on specific contexts of travel literature—the behavior of monkeys, the vileness of the Hottentots of South Africa—but here he deliberately desists from explicit comparisons. The word *human* directs the reader's imagination but a comparative descriptive equation is not fulfilled, and we are left wondering.

A horse appears, which scares off these marauding creatures, but this is no ordinary horse. When it encounters Gulliver, in one paragraph we find the following: "The Horse . . . looked full in my Face with man-

I ran to the body of a tree, and leaning my back against it, kept them off by waving my hanger

Illustration by Willy Pogány from *Gulliver's Travels*
(London: G. G. Harrap and Co., 1919).

ifest Tokens of Wonder . . . looking with a very mild Aspect . . . with Disdain, shook his Head, and Bent his Brows" (IV.i.226–27). When this horse is joined by another and they look "with great Earnestness" on Gulliver's face and hands, they are "surprized" at his hat, and look with "new Sighs of Wonder" (IV.i.227–28) at the lappet of his coat. Horses were the most familiar of animals in eighteenth-century town and country. Everyone would know that the expressiveness of a real horse's face was virtually limited to fear, as indicated by the flaring of nostrils. Modern techniques of cartoon animation in the cinema have accustomed audiences to humanized beasts, but eighteenth-century illustration of the horses in *Gulliver* is naturalistic—horses as horses. The evident comedy of Swift here, which he limits almost entirely to the first encounter in order not to overstate the point, is twofold. The reader attempts imaginative visualization and realizes how comically ludicrous the situation is, and/or accepts the description as a fantastic fiction since horses cannot express disdain, earnestness, etc. The circumspect reader suspends disbelief in order to relish the satire of the Yahoos and Houyhnhnms, which Gulliver quickly learns are the names of the animals and the horses.

REASON AND CLOTHING

The Houyhnhnms (vexatiously pronounced "Winnums" or "Winnims") are bemused by Gulliver's clothing. In each of the voyages Swift uses clothes to make a satirical point. On Lilliput, to make Gulliver new shirts, seamstresses measure by means of a cord that is then itself measured by an inch rule. Further, "Then they measured my right Thumb, and desired no more; for by a mathematical computation that twice round the Thumb is once round the Wrist, and so on to the Neck and the Waist . . . they fitted me exactly" (I.vi.51). The degree of error in the use of a Lilliputian ruler and the obviously false module make "exactly" very comic, but they also add to Swift's satirical conviction of the divorce between scientific theory and practical business. Glumdalclitch, Gulliver's nurse on Brobdingnag, also makes some shirts of the finest Brobdingnagian cloth, which feels "coarser than Sackcloth" (II.ii.86) to European skin. This is just a passing addition to the satire on relativity, whereas on Laputa Swift returns to mathematics. The Laputian tailor "first took my Altitude by a Quadrant, and then with Rule and Compasses, described the Dimensions and Outlines of my whole Body; all which he entered upon Paper, and in six Days brought my Cloths very ill made, and quite out of Shape, by happening to mistake a Figure in the Calculation" (III.ii.158). Commentators usually point to the notorious error of Newton's printer in adding a zero to his calculation of the distance of the sun. More generally, Swift is making a point about the factor of human error in science as well as ordinary life.

In the fourth voyage the role of clothing is altogether more extensive, central, and involved in relation to culture, philosophy, and satire. The discovery of Gulliver's lost hat by the Lilliputians offered, as we have seen, a major example of Swift's comic defamiliarization. It is Gulliver's hat and the skirts ("lappets") of his coat that give rise to the horses' surprise and wonder—particularly when the hat is removed and put back on. This detail is crucial to understanding Houyhnhnm reasoning and will be considered shortly. Meanwhile, Gulliver is escorted to the dwellings of the horses, acknowledging the rationality and order of their behavior and consequently expecting their masters to be the wisest people in the world. Unfortunately, Gulliver is taken to be a Yahoo, and when placed beside one of the beasts, he declares, "My Horror and Astonishment are not to be described, when I observed, in this abominable Animal, a perfect human Figure" (IV.ii.232). Though Gulliver makes the identification, in spite of a few differences, the Houyhnhnms are still puzzled by the clothing. This puzzlement leads to perplexity when Gulliver puts on his gloves and then removes them to gratify the bemused onlookers. (This also reveals an important point about Houyhnhnm reason.)

Gulliver discovers that the household he is introduced to is not presided over by a human but by a master Houyhnhnm. As Gulliver was surprised by the rational behavior of the horses, now they, in turn, "looked upon it as a Prodigy, that a brute Animal should discover such Marks of a rational Creature" (IV.iii.236). Like the other horses, the master Houyhnhnm "was most perplexed about my Cloaths, reasoning

sometimes with himself, whether they were a Part of my Body"
(IV.iii.236). This wonder is shared by visiting horses until Gulliver's
carefully preserved secret is revealed by way of a servant, when in
sleep his loose clothes fall aside and reveal his nakedness, and thus his
kinship with the foul Yahoo. As the pronunciation of his first word in
the Houyhnhnm language had declared him a Yahoo, so now as he
undresses in demonstration before the master, his Yahoo nature is con-
firmed, "he said, it was plain I must be a perfect *Yahoo*" (IV.iii.239).
Gulliver has explained to the master that in his home country everyone wears clothes according to the condition of the weather, but, more
important, because nature had taught humankind to cover organs of
sexuality. The master Houyhnhnm is at a complete loss to understand
this, wondering why "Nature [should] teach us to conceal what Nature
had given" (IV.iii.239). At this point one of the most important distinctions necessary for an understanding of part IV and all of *Gulliver's
Travels* needs to be made. It is a distinction that some commentators
seem unaware of, whereas others do not make it clear. When the master Houyhnhnm uses the words "nature" and "reason," he uses them
in a pagan, non-Christian sense, as debated in classical philosophy and
as reappeared in some utopian literature and in Deism. When Gulliver
uses these words, like Swift, he draws on meanings that derive from
their Christian, postlapsarian senses. Part of the inheritance of the Fall
of man was the sexual shame and guilt forever after symbolized by the
covering of genitals. Humankind acts according to a *fallen* nature that
is only redeemable by faith in Christ. Reason is flawed by sin. The
Houyhnhnms have no sense of this.

In his creation of the Houyhnhnms Swift synthesized many cultural factors that can be put up as signposts here. As horses, the
Houyhnhnms embody the ideal of *theriophily*—the animals' superiority over human beings. Their moral philosophy derives in large part
from Stoic rationalism, which to some degree is echoed in the rationalist Deism of the eighteenth century. The Houyhnhnms' society balances utopian elements from Plato, Plutarch, and Sir Thomas More.
From a textual or generic point of view the Houyhnhnms may be seen
as Swift's critique of seventeenth-century French Deist utopias: within
this critical position everything they say and do has a huge question

mark hanging over it, since they do not exist—they are unreal fictions serving the purpose of satire. Gulliver, in contrast, is real. Though indeed a fictive creation of Swift's for the purpose of satire, Gulliver has a relationship with the concrete actuality of history and society. Let us begin with the question of theriophily.

REASON AND THERIOPHILY

Theriophily derives initially from a non-Christian culture of early Cynic philosophy in which it was considered that the animals lived according to nature. Here nature and reason were manifestations of the same thing—the fundamental ordering principle of creation, call it God, the First Cause, the Logos, or what you will. Hence a paradox; though the animals were without reason, they lived according to nature, whereas human beings, who had inherited a portion of this reason, were often seen to abuse it. Human beings may become corrupt, but neither nature nor the animals are so.

Theriophily is a branch of primitivism. Primitivism takes the view that humankind has declined from an ideal standard. This took two forms, first the tradition of the Golden Age and associated ideas, which depicted humanity in harmony with nature—no winter, no war, no trade, but natural love, abundant food without labor, and amicable beasts. Second, another major tradition of primitivism was of man as a noble savage living in natural simplicity—taller, stronger, hunting for animals, enduring the hardness of the weather, and needing only the simplest of abodes. The development of towns and cities brought the effete corruption of so-called civilization. Luxury, vice, and crime rendered humanity corrupt in spirit, lewd in mind, and sick in body. The first kind of primitivism is often paralleled with the prelapsarian life in Eden before the Fall. In primitivism man falls and the seasons occur, in Christianity both man and nature fall. Theriophily evolved in disgust at fallen man's pride, a disgust that was trenchantly revived by Montaigne in the midst of the Renaissance celebration of humankind.[1]

The Houyhnhnms take to an extreme the theriophilists' notion, touched on in chapter 1 of this study, that when animals' behavior is studied closely it can be shown that they demonstrate some sort of reason. This is echoed throughout the fourth voyage, and the major statement appears in chapter VIII: "As these noble *Houyhnhnms* are endowed by Nature with a General Disposition to all Virtues, and have no Conception or Ideas of What is evil in a rational Creature; so their grand Maxim is, to cultivate *Reason,* and to be wholly governed by it" (IV.viii.272–73). Conversely, clothes could be taken to mean civilization, society, culture, and decency or a merely superficial covering, which, when removed, reveals how close humankind is to the animals. Faced with Edgar as Tom-o-Bedlam in the storm-wracked heath, King Lear confronts "the thing itself; unaccommodated man is no more but such a poor, bare, forked animal as thou art" (III.iv.109–11). Though the master Houyhnhnm concedes that Gulliver is cleaner and less "deformed" than the Yahoo, when it comes to real advantages he is much inferior. The nails on Gulliver's fore and hind feet are useless: walking on two feet only is unstable; the flatness of his face means that he cannot see either side without turning the head; he can't eat without lifting food to the mouth; his hind feet are too soft, with unnecessary "clefts and divisions" (toes); his whole body needs a covering against heat and cold (IV.iv.244–45).

It is tempting to call this a blinkered view. Swift's dialectical subtlety here is at its finest. Swift bends some standard theriophilist arguments toward an implicit critique of the horses in their inability to consider any criterion other than horsey norms. Yet this satirically reflects how humankind, the paragon of creation, always imposes its so-called superior values on the chain of being. Again, the focus of the master's argument—the particular inferiority of Gulliver's fore and hind feet—brings to mind several contrasting and contradictory things that will be examined when we turn from the horses' critique of their guest to Swift's satire on the horses.

Gulliver's experience before the King of Brobdingnag is now reversed. He then espoused a Whig encomiastic ideology, which was subsequently taken apart by the ruler. As Gulliver experienced a huge reversal from giant to pygmy, now the world is turned upside down as he recounts the relationship between human and horse in England. The popular satiric tradition of *mundus inversus,* or "The World

Upside Down," is found in chapbooks and broadsheets throughout Western culture, including two English chapbooks of the early eighteenth century.[2] The world upside down reverses natural and social order and hierarchy and can be interpreted in reactionary or radical ways. Does obvious absurdity buttress the status quo or suggest that the status quo itself is absurd?

Swift's play on the topic of inversion is extremely sophisticated. When the master Houyhnhnm initially hears from Gulliver how in England Yahoo grooms wait on and pamper horses, this is all right and proper from the Houyhnhnm point of view. But when Gulliver goes on to explain the functions of the horse in English society, including "drawing Chariots" (IV.iv.243), the master is outraged. Conversely, Swift supplies the conventional image of the world upside down: "About Noon I saw coming towards the House a Kind of Vehicle, drawn like a Sledge by four *Yahoos*. There was in it an old Steed, who seemed to be of Quality" (IV.ii.233). But of greater significance, which will be developed shortly, is Swift's separation and inversion of the physical and intellectual faculties that make man what he is—*animal rationale*, a rational animal. The profound importance of this phrase will be a central consideration. As Gulliver explains, with some trepidation, concerning his recent misadventure at sea: "the Ship was made by Creatures like myself, who in all the Countries I had travelled, as well as in my own, were the only governing, rational Animals; and that upon my Arrival hither, I was as much astonished to see the Houyhnhnms act like rational Beings, as he or his Friends could be in finding some Marks of Reason in a Creature he was pleased to call a *Yahoo;* to which I owned my Resemblance in every Part, but could not account for their degenerate and brutal Nature" (IV.iii.241).

GULLIVER'S ENGLAND

Gulliver's account to his master of his misfortune with the pirates inadvertently offers a prefatory summary of vice and crime for what follows in the account of England—in effect, the ship of state is ruled by a bunch of "pirates" vitiated by "the Desire of Power and Riches . . . the

CHAPTER II

Illustration by Willy Pogány from *Gulliver's Travels* (London: G. G. Harrap and Co., 1919).

terrible Effects of Lust, Intemperance, Malice, and Envy" (IV.iv.246). In the following account of diplomacy and war, Swift's technique is overt yet subtle. On the one hand, Gulliver as Swift's persona voices a diametric irony, on the other, Gulliver as character is shown as approaching the extremes of disillusion with humanity, one step from final misanthropy.

For diametric irony, consider the following:

> It is a very justifiable Cause of War to invade a Country after the People have been wasted by Famine, destroyed by Pestilence, or embroiled by Factions amongst themselves. It is justifiable to enter into a War against our nearest Ally, when one of his Towns lies convenient for us, or a Territory of Land, that would render our Dominions round and compact. If a Prince send Forces into a Nation, where the People are poor and ignorant, he may lawfully put half of them to Death and make Slaves of the rest, in order to civilize and reduce them from their barbarous Way of Living. (IV.v.249)

The "justifiable" is stripped of the rationalizing euphemism of diplomacy and seen for what it is: Reason of State and Realpolitik are just abstract shields for inhuman opportunism and blatant crime. "Civilize" and "reduce" (convert) are colonialist sanctions for "lawful" plunder, torture, rape, and massacre.

In response to this the master Houyhnhnm makes a distinction between the behavior of his Yahoos and that described in Gulliver's account of the English and European species. The Yahoos cannot be blamed for acting according to their bestial Yahoo nature, "But, when a Creature, pretending to Reason, could be capable of such Enormities, he dreaded lest the Corruption of that Faculty might be worse than Brutality itself" (IV.v.251). Gulliver continues his account of England. Justice is subverted by the professional practices of lawyers, who turn it into a criminal conspiracy against the innocent. Money had subverted hereditary society, creating the extremes of poverty and luxury and consequent immorality. And from luxury comes all the sicknesses that plague humankind. Corruption spreads to the body politic, by which the great chain of being had been displaced by the chain of patronage and placemen. Idleness, luxury, and inbreeding had corrupted a nobility now incapable of its hereditary duties. Again, such revelations provoke a similar response: "[H]e looked upon us as a sort of Animals to whose Share, by what Accident he could not conjecture, some small Pittance of *Reason* had fallen, whereof we made no other Use than by its Assistance to aggravate our *natural* Corruptions, and to acquire new ones which Nature had not given us." The master Houyhnhnm summarizes: "[O]ur Institutions of *Government* and *Law* were plainly owing to our gross Defects in *Reason,* and by consequence, in *Virtue;* because *Reason* alone is sufficient to govern a *Rational* Creature; which was therefore a Character we had no Pretence to Challenge"—that is, lay claim to (IV.vii.263–64).

The master Houyhnhnm's fuller response, which Gulliver summarizes, is much more crushing. The account of England has convinced him that Gulliver's species are alike in mind as well as body. A reductive catalogue follows, in which human activities are reflected by the Yahoos, the veneer of culture removed, just as the removal of Gulliver's clothes had shown his greater resemblance to those animals. Even with sufficient provision the Yahoo would fight for the food of others, would fight other groups, or would fight among themselves—all without cause. Yahoo avarice led to the hoarding of "certain *shining Stones*" (IV.vii.265), which in turn led to theft and fighting even though the stones had no practical use. Appetite and aggression seemed the two motivating factors of Yahoo existence, except when relieved by the drunkenness produced by sucking a juicy root.

Yahoo herds were controlled by a ruling Yahoo and his favorite, "whose Employment was to *lick his Master's Feet and Posteriors, and drive the Female Yahoos to his Kennel*" (IV.vii.267). Elsewhere, the females and males fought among themselves, the females clearly showing signs of a coquetry and salaciousness recognizable in English society. Ironically, the Yahoos seem marginally superior to humans in that they only have one illness, the spleen, and have not cultivated sexual perversions. Swift cleverly follows this with the incident of a young female Yahoo making sexual advances on Gulliver as he bathes in the nude, which precipitates a major turning point. "For now I could no longer deny, that I was a real *Yahoo,* in every Limb and Feature since the Females had a natural Propensity to me as one of their own Species" (IV.viii.272). Eventually, Gulliver's devotion to the Houyhnmhnms impels him to an all-encompassing judgment:

> When I thought of my Family, my Friends, my Countrymen, or human Race in general, I considered them as they really were, *Yahoos* in Shape and Disposition, perhaps a little more civilized, and qualified with the Gift of Speech; but making no other Use of Reason, than to improve and multiply those Views, whereof their Brethren in this Country had only the Share that Nature allotted them. When I happened to behold the Reflection of my own Form in a Lake or Fountain, I turned away my Face in Horror and detestation of my self. (IV.x.386)

But it is the Houyhnhnms who have held the mirror up to Gulliver's apparent nature. The word *Houyhnhnm* in their language signifies a horse. Etymologically, it means "the Perfection of Nature" (IV.iii.237). What does that "perfection" consist of? What is it, exactly, that has deranged Gulliver?

THE HORSE UTOPIA

As in the collectivist ethics of More's *Utopia,* the Houyhnhnms promote friendship and benevolence, thus "home" is everywhere since they have an unceremonious respect for each other, and even for strangers, which subsumes the familial. Temperance and industry, exercise and cleanliness are the rule for both sexes, who share an identical education. Spartan hardihood is developed in the exercises of youth. As in Plato's *Republic,* marriage is based on eugenic lines, not romance. Strength and beauty are brought together to forestall degeneration of the race, not to foster amatory individualism. Sexual morality is natural, not enforced. Childbearing is limited by the social program, though couples may provide colts or foals for others when necessary. Sex is for the purpose of controlling population; sexual passion is not known. As the Spartans had a slave "helot" underclass, so the Houyhnhnms have an inferior caste of servant-horses. These are naturally inferior, docile, and unaspiring from birth. Beneath these are the bestial Yahoos, who are confined to the fields as a cross between slave and draught animal. Swift differs fundamentally from More's *Utopia* in this. All utopian citizens engaged in agricultural work, but the high-caste Houyhnhnms, like Plato's rulers and Sparta's aristocracy, are above laboring.[3]

Surprisingly, in view of these facts, we are told that the Houyhnhnm language has no words for "Power, Government, War, Law, Punishment, and a Thousand other things" (IV.iv.246). The simple, modest culture of the Houyhnhnms consists of traditional knowledge and oral poetry, like that of the Spartans, since they have no conception of printed literature. The poetry celebrates their culture, in praise of such things as friendship or victory in games. Though we are told that "their Language expressed the Passions very well" (IV.i.228), elsewhere we learn that "their Wants and Passions are fewer than among us" (IV.iv.244). "Fewer" appears to be an understatement, since upon death friends and relations express "neither Joy nor Grief at their Departure" (IV.ix.281). From this it would seem that the Houyhnhnms are a race of four-legged Stoics, which brings us to their philosophy.

Houyhnhnm belief has been made indirectly apparent throughout the fourth voyage in the horses' criticism of Gulliver. Reason and nature are its obvious bases. The following quotations are gathered together here as the five main statements recorded by Gulliver, the worshipping acolyte. First, "Nature and Reason were sufficient Guides for a reasonable Animal" (IV.v.252). Second, "Reason alone is sufficient to govern a *Rational* Creature" (IV.vii.263). Referred to earlier, the third quotation deserves lengthier citation since it contains several ideas, some of which will form the basis of my interpretation of the fourth book and thus of *Gulliver's Travels* as a whole, as well as the basis of a critique of much of the "hard" school of criticism.

As these noble Houyhnhnms are endowed by Nature with a general Disposition to all Virtues, and have no Conceptions or Ideas of what is evil in a rational Creature; so their grand Maxim is, to cultivate *Reason,* and to be wholly governed by it. Neither is *Reason* among them a Point problematical as with us, where Men can argue with Plausibility on both Sides of a Question; but strikes you with immediate Conviction; as it must needs do when it is not mingled, obscured, or discoloured by Passion and Interest. I remember it was with extreme Difficulty that I could bring my Master to understand the Meaning of the Word *Opinion,* or how a point could be disputable; because *Reason* taught us to affirm or deny only where we are certain; and beyond our Knowledge we cannot do either. (IV.vii.272–73)

Fourth, the master cannot understand Gulliver's account of human illness because "Nature . . . worketh all things to Perfection" (IV.vi.257). Last, we are reminded in chapter IX that the Houyhnhnms are "naturally disposed to every Virtue [and] wholly governed by Reason" (IV.ix.279).

The rationalism espoused by the horses is the foundation for a utopian political philosophy combining Sir Thomas More, Plato, and Plutarch and for a moral philosophy deriving from Stoicism and subsequently from the principles of the religion of Deism. Utopianism has been touched on. The central tenet of Stoicism was to live in conformity with reason and nature; this is the highest good, which is in part attained by resisting and containing irrational emotions. Immediately it can be seen that the Houyhnhnms' Stoicism is something of a travesty, since they don't have any emotions to resist (apart from one that they nurture—hatred of the Yahoos). Further, Stoicism recognized moral evil as deriving from the intention of humankind. The Houyhnhnms simplistic deficiency here will be examined as a foundation of Swift's satire. Houyhnhnm society, however, reflects Stoic thought in the absolute distinction between the virtuous and the vicious, between horse and Yahoo. As in the text of St. Paul, which began this chapter, Stoicism divided humankind into the wise and the foolish. The etymology of Houyhnhnm as "perfection of nature" fulfills the Stoic ideal of the wise individual, but this was the rare ideal. General depravity was the norm—thus the irony in Swift's presentation of a *race* of Stoics. St. Augustine recognized how close the Stoic doctrine of folly was to the Christian doctrine of the unregenerate—those incapable of spiritual rebirth and renewal. In the Houyhnhnms and Yahoos Swift dichotomizes Stoic wisdom and the Christian concept of the body's unregenerate depravity. From a Christian point of view both are equally removed from the truths of the Gospels.

The critical issue concerning just how far the Houyhnhnms' belief presents a satire on Deism is not usually pressed today. Around the 1950s it was an assumption held by leading authorities like Irvin Ehrenpreis and Kathleen Williams.[4] Ehrenpreis considered that *Gulliver's Travels* reflected Swift's distaste for the Deism of Bolingbroke, whose correspondence with the author at that time espoused his beliefs. Swift actually named one of his horses Bolingbroke. Williams took the view that *Gulliver* might well be a reply to the explicit Deist, anti-Christian utopias of Vairesse and Foigny in the preceding century. In contrast, a later commentator claims that if we look at *Gulliver's Travels* on its own there is no internal evidence that indicates a concern with Christianity or that suggests the author was even a Christian at all.[5]

The argument cannot be resolved with hard-and-fast evidence one way or another, but the following points are offered in the belief that one of Swift's primary satirical targets was rationalism, and at the time it would not have been possible to read passages like those quoted immediately above without associating Houyhnhnm and deist reason. Before proceeding, a brief analogy may be considered. At a time when the American people were going through the trauma of the Vietnam war, two films appeared, *Soldier Blue* (1970) and *Little Big Man* (1970). The films were concerned with incidents in which the massacre of Indians took place in the setting of nineteenth-century America. But the films were taken by everyone as an indirect comment on the revelation of the U.S. massacre of Vietnamese, most notoriously, for instance, at My Lai in 1968. In the language of the day, the word or image of *massacre* in one context was ineluctably evoked by another. By the 1720s the language of polemical religious debate was such that a semantic overlap in the word *reason* took place. Anthony Collins, in his *A Discourse of Free-Thinking* (1713), offered the premise "whosoever live by reason are Christians."[6] This might not square with the facts of Swift's narrative, but it is the clear logical implication of Collins's proposition: Houyhnhnms live by reason, therefore they are deist Christians.

In *Gulliver's Travels* Swift does not engage in doctrinal debate concerning the deist rejection of Christian mystery and miracles, like those of the Trinity and the Resurrection. These are considered in his sermon "On the Trinity." Swift takes a satirical edge to the root of Deism. Cut through rationalism and the rest must fall. Beast utopias are rare, and the absurdity of conferring reason on antipodean quadrupeds seems a direct slap in the face of the seventeenth-century utopias of Foigny and Vairasse. These did not use the notion of ideal societies as innately satirical by reflecting on the actual but used remote Australian settings to promulgate a religion of Deism freed from any pretensions to Christianity whatsoever. Pierre Bayle, in the ninth volume of *A General Dictionary, Historical and Critical* (1739), saw quite clearly the implications of Foigny's pre-Adamic dating of the origin of his ideal hermaphrodites: it was "designed to insinuate, that these people did not descend from Adam but from an Hermaphrodite, who did not fall like him from a state of innocence." In Foigny we find that pigs are used to plough up the ground, which appears to be a source much closer than anything else suggested for the comparable suggestion in the grand academy of Lagado. On the other hand, Vairasse's Governor of Sporounde sounds very much like a Houyhnhnm when he "exhorts" strangers to "moderation" and "virtue" (Atkinson, 76, 102).

In the context of Foigny's pre-Adamic idealism, Swift's Yahoos can be considered as symbolizing the Fall. They stand in direct opposition to the Houyhnhnms' representation of the logical extreme of benevolists' optimism, which bypassed original sin and human corruption. To quote once more, the Houyhnhnms "have no Conceptions or Ideas of what is evil in a rational Creature" (IV.viii.272). R. M. Frye's valuable research, cited earlier, shows that in addition to drawing on travelers' accounts of monkeys and primitive peoples Swift with some deliberation drew on the Bible and homiletic tradition for his Christian symbols of sin. Swift's language of filth, corruption, and deformity when describing the Yahoos echoes that of theological condemnation in which all physical depravity symbolized the corruption of sin. From Frye's research it appears that Swift went out of his way to specifically align the Yahoos' diet with the prohibited pollution of defilement as expounded in Leviticus: asses' flesh, dead cows, putrefying meat, other carrion, cats and dogs, weasels and rats. Summarizing, Frye writes: "The Yahoo is that fleshly element in human nature which cannot be disavowed, which may in fact degrade humankind to the level of the brute beasts, and which vitiates any argument for the self-redemptive power of human reason and the final efficacy of natural benevolence" (208). In one of Swift's conjectured origins for the creation of the Yahoo, from "corrupted Mud and Slime" (IV.ix.277), he turned not to Genesis and the creation of Adam but to an early mythographer, Hyginus, and his fable CCXX, as rendered by Robert Burton in the *Anatomy of Melancholy*. "Dame *Cura* by chance went over a brook, and, taking up some of the dirty slime, made an image of it . . . his name shall be *Homo ab humo.*" The pejorative edge of Burton's diction adds emphasis to the "corruption" Swift applied to Hyginus's "mud."[7] Steward Lacasce, in a most perceptive comment, notes that the Yahoos illustrate six of the seven deadly sins—covetousness, lust, anger, gluttony, envy, sloth—while Gulliver embodies the seventh, pride, by the end of the work.[8]

This moral and biblical perspective on the Yahoos brings their significance into focus. But what of the Houyhnhnms? By and large Swift's satirical method is dialectical here, as it is in the work as a whole. In their response to Gulliver's account of England, the Houyhnhnms reinforce the satire on the home country. When we turn to the question of whether the Houyhnhnms offer a utopian ideal in themselves, however, they become an additional object of satire. The leading question then arises, are the Houyhnhnm virtues of no significance at all? Are we finally faced with something that goes beyond misanthropy and cynicism—an ultimate nihilism? The close of this chapter will attempt to answer these questions.

REASON AND DYSTOPIA

Most critics recognize that the Houyhnhnms' reason is often less than perfect, though there has never been a systematic study of the subject. The following analysis offers some additional details to those usually cited, and goes further in exposing the inner contradiction of

Houyhnhnm knowledge, an aspect of Swift's intellectual wit behind the overt comedy of the fourth voyage.

The horses are initially puzzled by Gulliver's clothes and hat, even though he removes the latter and then puts it back on. This bafflement is repeated in the master Houyhnhnm's household as, we are told, "they had no Conception" (IV.ii.232) of clothes in spite of the earlier removal of the hat. Though "reasoning sometimes with himself [the master] was most perplexed about my Cloaths" (IV.iii.236), yet he had witnessed Gulliver's demonstration of removing them and putting them back on again (IV.ii.234). The Houyhnhnms are incapable of making a simple logical deduction from hat and gloves to Gulliver's other clothes; as they are evidently coverings for head and hands, so his coat is a covering for the body. They cannot resolve the issue by inference, and lateral thought is well beyond them—that is, they understand the concept of using a covering to protect themselves from the elements as their houses have roofs, but they are unable to reason analogously to explain clothing.

As we have seen, an extensive theriophilic criticism of Gulliver's "fore feet" is made in comparison with those of the horses and Yahoos. Yet in some detail Gulliver tells us how he resolved his predicament concerning food following the master Houyhnhnm's concern about his hunger, after his repulsion at the offer of Yahoo food, and distaste for that of the horses (IV.ii.234–35). The horse orders a servant to bring the traveler some oats, and, presumably before the master Houyhnhnm's eyes, these Gulliver heats, rubs to remove the husks, winnowing the grain which is ground and beaten to flour by stones, then kneaded into a paste with water, shaped into cakes and toasted before the fire—all with his hands. Furthermore, Gulliver makes traps from Yahoo hairs to catch rabbits and birds, gathers herbs, and makes butter—all with his hands. In spite of this evidence of human resourcefulness and dexterity, the master Houyhnhnm blindly applies a priori reasoning from evidence of horse and Yahoo physiology. Swift was obviously struck by the opportunity offered for a broader burlesque humor in this, given the familiarity of the horse: "The Houyhnhnms use the hollow Part between the Pastern and the Hoof of their Fore-feet, as we do our Hands, and this with greater

Dexterity, than I could at first imagine. I have seen a white Mare of our Family thread a Needle (which I lent her on Purpose) with that Joynt. They milk their Cows, reap their Oats, and do all the Work which requires Hands, in the same Manner" (IV.ix.280).

Swift chooses just about the most precise and dexterous of eighteenth-century domestic activities, combined with the narrator's awed veracity of empirical observation, to remind the reader of folly and wisdom in reading circumspectly—and to provide a celebrated humorous incident that, as indicated here, contributes to an ultimately serious point. In the same context, we hear, "They have a Kind of Tree, which at Forty Years old loosens in the Root, and falls with the first Storm; it grows very strait, and being pointed like Stakes with a sharp Stone . . . they stick them erect in the Ground. . . . They have a Kind of hard Flints, which by grinding against other Stones, they form into Instruments that serve instead of Wedges, Axes, and Hammers" (IV.ix.280). This passage shows that if needs be, the Houyhnhnms are capable of boat building, which is indeed the case when the sorrel nag undertakes most of the labor to build Gulliver's vessel. This is inconsistent with the master Houyhnhnm's earlier assertion: "He knew it was impossible that there could be a Country beyond the Sea, or that a Parcel of Brutes could move a wooden Vessel whither they pleased upon Water. He was sure no *Houyhnhnm* alive could make such a Vessel" (IV.iii.237). The master doubly contradicts himself in this passage, since in the grand debate at the general assembly of the horses he reminds the audience of Yahoo origins: "He . . . affirmed that the two *Yahoos* said to be first seen among them, had been driven thither over the Sea" (IV.ix.278). A simple inference is that they came from another land, which is denied as "impossible."

Putting the Yahoo origins aside, Gulliver himself stands before the Houyhnhnm master as a kind of evidence of the contrary. Moreover, what kind of evidence has led to that "impossible"? No exploration is mentioned. Therefore a more accurate and logical statement would be, "It is not known that . . ." or "There is no evidence that . . ." The master's statement is opinion hardened into dogma, yet elsewhere it is claimed that the horses do not know the meaning of "opinion." In denying evidence, he is irrational. The Houyhnhnms' identification of

Gulliver with the Yahoo and similarly Gulliver's self-identification with that creature are both examples of one of the commonest fallacies—*secundem quid*. Both disallow the greater dissimilarity and reach a conclusion based on lesser likenesses, even though both have examined the contrary evidence over a great period of time. The inconsistencies of the Houyhnhnms are such that, even allowing for small slips, Swift must have carefully planned them.

Of Houyhnhnm speech, we hear, "Power, Government, War, Law, Punishment, and a Thousand other Things had no Terms, wherein that Language could express them" (IV.iv.246–47). Power is exercised continually to keep the Yahoos subservient, and the lower-class servant-horses are docilely inferior in every way. The grand assembly appears to be a form of Republican government that always debates the question of punishing the Yahoos with extermination. Law is unnecessary, because there is absolute conformity, and, though there is no war, at the debate the horses show their concern that Gulliver may be an insurrectionary who will lead the Yahoos in civil rebellion. Furthermore, the practice of the debate seems to conflict directly with the ground of Houyhnhnm reason: "Neither is *Reason* among them a Point problematical as with us, as it must needs do where it is not mingled, obscured or discoloured by Passion and Interest" (IV.viii.273). Gulliver's words describe precisely the nature of the Houyhnhnms' debate, including their single all-consuming passion, hatred of the Yahoos. It would appear that in this passionless race, at the grand assembly, reason divides but hatred unites. Such contradictions in Houyhnhnm thought and society imply that the horses' beliefs are founded on self-deception, *the thing which was not.*

The thing which was not is the circumlocution that is used, since the concepts of lying, doubting, or not believing are little known or understood by the Houyhnhnms (IV.iv.242). On the surface Swift uses a broad joke, since it is obviously the Houyhnhnm—a rational horse—that is *the thing which was not.* Elsewhere the master Houyhnhnm agrees to keep the secret of Gulliver's clothes—which is to be prepared to lie in principle. And we learn later that he has kept the truth from Gulliver of the decree of the general assembly. *The thing which was not* is the linguistic pinprick on which the Houyhnhnm utopia implodes. The phrase does not lend support to their honesty but to their negativity, limitation, and unreality. As Ludwig Wittgenstein puts it, "the limits of my language mean the limits of my world."[9] How can the Houyhnhnms have an understanding of honesty and truth if they have no conception of deception and lying? Of what value are their virtues if they have no experience of vice? Knowledge derives from overlapping semantic fields. It is not possible to come to an understanding of good without at the same time developing a knowledge of evil—at least within the real, fallen, world of experience.

Milton gave voice to humankind's essential postlapsarian situation—"Knowledge of Good bought dear by knowing ill" (*Paradise Lost*, IV.222). *Houyhnhnm* might well signify "the perfection of nature" in the Houyhnhnm language of utopian society, but in its translation into the real world it is seen for what it is, an arrogant and naive contradiction in terms. The limitations of Houyhnhnm society are often mentioned: its conformity, dullness, and joylessness. But the dualistic disabling factor is their lack of love and ignorance of evil. Take love out of human experience and a Cartesian automaton is left. Love is the center from which all affirmative values radiate—affection, tenderness, care, concern, regard, selflessness, and so on. And there are those for whom life without love of one's country or love of God would be inconceivable. That is to say, without love, there can be no real value. From a Christian point of view, understanding of evil is inseparable from good—God, love, truth, virtue. The Houyhnhnms only understand evil or badness in terms of Yahoo nature, just as in other societies at certain moments of history a ruling class has determined that the "other" is the source of all corruption and evil—black people, Gypsies, Armenians, Jews. Thus arises the dystopian specter of totalitarianism in Houyhnhnm society, combining communist and fascist factors. All horses are equal but some are more equal than others. For Swift, in the real world all men are equally fallen.

What, then, can be said for Houyhnhnm virtue, and why is it that many considerable critics and scholars have felt that the Houyhnhnms offer a positive ideal? The issue can be put simply. If virtues such as friendship, benevolence, cleanliness, and temperance are abstracted from the book *Gulliver's Travel* and we are asked, are these admirable or not, the answer is almost certainly to be in the affirmative since loneliness, selfishness, dirtiness, and drunkenness are usually considered unattractive, to say the least. Judgment is within a scale of experiential relativities open to choice. Put these qualities back into the book and choice is lost because in Houyhnhnm society generally there is no individual will, only submission to a collective public ideology. From this point of view the fallacy of arguing that the virtues Swift admired in the sextumvirate on Glubbdubdrib are found in the Houyhnhnms—therefore the horses represent ideals—is plain to see. For example, Sir Thomas More's integrity was tested by putting his head on the block. Death means nothing to the Houyhnhnms, and choice seems limited to something like hot or cold milk with their oats. Their integrity is nominal only, an artificial fabrication, like their utopia, and meant to be seen as such, Houyhnhnm reason included.

When man fell he did not become a brute like the Yahoo, though he was subject to brutalizing passions like hatred and blood-lust. In his mixed nature, man retained the vestiges of prelapsarian reason. Hence arose the commonplace definition bearing witness to the human being's paradoxical nature, *homo est animal rational*. In his two most famous letters concerning *Gulliver's Travels,* Swift confronted this question. On 29 September 1725, Swift wrote to Pope, "I have got Materials Towards a Treatis proving the falsity of that Definition *animal rationale;* and to show it should be only *rationis capax*. Upon this great foundation of Misanthropy (though not Timon's matter) The whole building of my Travells is erected" (*Correspondence,* 3:103). The passage immediately preceding this needs to be quoted to help interpret Swift's comments. Swift protests that humankind in the collective, aggregate sense—"Nations professions and Communityes"—he has always hated, whereas his love is toward individuals. He continues, "principally I hate and detest that animal called man, although I hartily love John, Peter, Thomas and so forth" (*Correspondence,* 3:103). Two months later, on 26 November 1725, Swift wrote again to Pope, seemingly correcting the last statement: "I tell you after all that I do not hate Mankind, it is vous autres who hate them because you would have them reasonable Animals, and are Angry for being disappointed. I have always rejected that Definition and made another of my own" (*Correspondence*, 3:118).

"Man is a rational animal" was a definition formulated in antiquity and taken over by Christian culture. The pagan idea fitted the dualistic conception of fallen man as a compound of reason and passion, mind and body. By Swift's time, the "animal" part of the phrase had almost dropped off, like the tail from the evolutionary human body. The combined influences of optimistic humanism, progressivism, benevolism, neo-Stoicism, and Deism led to the conception of the human being as a solely rational being. Swift's "rationis capax"—capable of reason—brings home human limitation. Reason is not denied but seen for what it is in view of actual human conduct. Swift acknowledged that his concept of misanthropy was not fashioned after Timon of Athens, whose passionate rage against ingratitude was the vitriol of a self-consuming ego. Swift uses misanthropy as the investigative tool of the probing satirist. Individuals are loved, anything else leads to labels, which individuals can hide behind; then generalized misrepresentations on the idea of human being begin. Look at an individual and you can see what he or she adds up to. Accept a label like "man is a rational animal" and deception creeps in. Swift knows that humankind is an aggregate of individuals, with all their shortcomings. Those who, like Pope, foolishly expect the fallible individual to live up to an unrealistic ideal will always be "disappointed."

Swift's sermon "On the Trinity" defends orthodox Anglicanism against Deism, arguing for the limitation of reason in questions of faith and doctrine but acknowledging "that every Man is bound to follow the Rules and Directions of that Measure of Reason which God hath given him" (*Prose Works*, 9:109). Again, "It is the mistake of wise and good men that they expect more Reason and Virtue from human nature, than taking it in the bulk, it is in any sort capable of" (*Prose Works*, 5:78). Gulliver has taken as his "measure" supreme Houyhnhnm reason, and as a consequence has violently reversed the optimistic expectation of a "wise and good man" by expecting Yahoo brutalism only.

R. S. Crane has shown, unsurprisingly, that Swift and his contemporaries at the university would have faced that definition *homo est animal rationale*.[10] In the textbooks of logic, irrational animal was opposed to man, and Crane discovered that a frequently named contrast was the horse. The distinguishing characteristic of the horse is its whinnying—*equus est animal hinnibile.* Some critics speculate that the name Houyhnhnm might derive from *hinnibile.* But this is a minor point. Crane immediately grasped the design of Swift's satirical strategy in the fourth voyage. Swift reverses the commonplaces behind the logic. *Rational* and *animal* are divided and reversed. Rationality is given to an animal, the horse, and animality is given to the Yahoo. The Houyhnhnm name, if we remove some whinnying sounds and make a slight reversal (Hounum—Humun), becomes a distortion of *human,* while the Yahoo, as we have seen, are a physical distortion of human beings. Gulliver is the middle term, fallen humanity combining the complexity of reason and emotion, virtues and vices, which is man's lot to recognize and control.

Thus the interpretation of part IV so far follows that of the "soft" school of criticism. The Houyhnhnms are satirized as false ideals in a false utopia, and Gulliver is brought down by self-deluding pride. An implication here, however, is that those learned commentators who adhere to the "hard" school point of view are themselves taken in by the horses. The final chapter will consider this approach and in turn offer a reinterpretation that goes beyond the limits of both schools.

10

The Closing Satirical Frame

The general assembly decides that Gulliver should be banished from Houyhnhnmland. Since Gulliver's master has a number of arguments that bring him to the opposite conclusion, Houyhnhnm reason is no longer unanimous, though there is no evidence that the master offered these arguments at the grand debate. He believes that Gulliver's imitation of the Houyhnhnms has got rid of some Yahoo traits and made him suitable for service, whereas the assembly fears the effects of Gulliver's reason if he is relegated to Yahoo status. For all the rationality of the horse society, its members don't appear to see the possibilities of breeding a more tractable slave-class from Gulliver, given their own eugenic practices. Neither do they see the possibilities of Gulliver's account of castration of horses in England. Applied to Yahoos, this could be used either to render the males docile or to gradually exterminate the species. Even the adoring traveler feels "yet in my weak and corrupt Judgement I thought it might consist with Reason to have been less rigorous" (IV.x.287) than drowning, which would in all likelihood result from the assembly's exhortation that he "swim back to the Place from whence [he] came" (IV.x.286).

Gulliver nonetheless builds a vessel in preparation for banishment with the help of the sorrel nag, who shows a little moral revisionism in his "Tenderness" for the sailor (IV.x.288). At this point Swift slips in a seemingly innocent symbol of Houyhnhnm limitation. After climbing a height, Gulliver says, "[I] fancied I saw a small Island, towards the *North-East:* I took out my Pocket-glass, and could then distinguish it about five Leagues off . . . but it appeared to the Sorrel Nag to be only a blue Cloud: For, as he had no Conception of any Country beside his own, so he could not be as expert in distinguishing remote Objects at Sea, as we who so much converse in that Element" (IV.x.288–89). This is a perfect image for the physical and mental insularity of the Houyhnhnms, in which human sight and technology triumph over horse myopia. Swift leaves the reader to make this distinction, since Gulliver, in spite of his banishment, is a Houyhnhnm manqué and a misanthropic hater of the Yahoo-human race, beginning with himself, as attested in his reaction of "Horror and detestation" on seeing his reflection in the water (IV.x.286). But it is important to note that what might be considered tragic, serious, or certainly noncomic in the last three chapters is almost always juxtaposed against something that considerably modifies, and thus mixes, the tone. Immediately following Gulliver's confession of disgust on seeing his own image, for instance, we find the following passage: "By conversing with the Houyhnhnms, and looking upon them with Delight, I fell to imitate their Gait and Gesture, which is now grown into a Habit; and my friends often tell me in a blunt Way, that I *trot like a Horse;* which, however, I take for a great Compliment: Neither shall I disown, that in speaking I am apt to fall into the Voice and manner of the *Houyhnhnms,* and hear my self ridiculed on that Account without the least Mortification" (IV.x.286).

Eventually, the wounded Gulliver escapes savage natives to be taken up by Portuguese Yahoos. The Swift-Gulliver dialectic takes an unusual narratological turn here. *Gulliver's Travels* ends with the traveler's misanthropy unpalliated: back in England, contemplating the English "*Yahoo*-kind," he says, "when I behold a Lump of Deformity, and Diseases both in Body and Mind, smitten with *Pride,* it immediately breaks all the Measures of my Patience" (IV.xii.304). Given such an extreme misanthropy, which colors the whole of the last two chapters, it seems unlikely that, in terms of psychological naturalism, Gulliver would have been able to perceive the humane kindliness of Pedro de Mendez, the captain who rescues him. To make a moral and satirical point of the greatest significance, Swift still uses the first-person voice of Gulliver to express something more suited to an omniscient third-person narrator. What is being said is not ironic and thus does not use the ventriloquial mask technique. This narrative stance is unique in *Gulliver's Travels;* quotations from the book will help to reveal it.

Gulliver says of the Portuguese sailors, "They spoke to me with great Humanity" (IV.xi.294), and of the captain, "he was a very courteous and generous Person" (IV.xi.295); yet, "I was ready to faint at the very Smell of him and his Men" (IV.xi.295). Gulliver condescends to treat Mendez as "an Animal which had some little Portion of Reason" (IV.ix.295), blighted by "the Corruption of his Nature" (IV.ix.296). Then, in the very next sentence, we find, "The Captain, a wise Man." The dichotomous mode discloses the workings of the dialectic as Swift anticipates the conclusion in which it will be halted at a point of mutual extremity between satirist and reformer/travel writer. Captain Mendez has an importance in criticism of *Gulliver's Travels* well beyond his narrative status as the means of returning home this misanthropic survivor. Mendez shows a humane patience, tolerance, and consideration of his troubled guest. He shows gentlemanly civility in treating Gulliver as an equal, and provides food, clothing, and security in his own house after disembarking at Lisbon. But Gulliver's Houyhnhnm values see all in black-and-white terms, horse or animal. Reverting to his mixed mode of satirist-persona, Swift packs much of the irony of part IV into one italicized word: Gulliver is finally persuaded to concede, "his whole Deportment was so obliging, added to very good *human* Understanding, that I really began to tolerate his Company" (IV.ix.297). There is probably no other writer in the English language who could achieve so much in one word. That use of *human* indicates both Gulliver's horsey condescension and proud contempt as well as Swift's vindication of human values. Captain Mendez becomes a welcoming beacon of humanity as Gulliver's irony rebounds against himself and Houyhnhnm limitation. The "hard" school of interpretation, however, sees things altogether differently.

Gulliver, the mad misanthropist in despair at humankind, is seen as a tragic figure. The Houyhnhnms offered a vision of perfection, a benign utopia, against the realities of so-called civilization—vice, crime, and animality—which palls in comparison. For the "hard" school Captain Mendez is simply discounted as a member of the Yahoo race. This approach tends to re-read the fourth voyage backward, from the final position of Gulliver's alienation. Comedy and satire are largely put aside in response to the shock of Gulliver's final condition. Concepts, thoughts, and ideas surrender to the critics' feelings. The spectacle of such a madman is disturbingly serious. Emotion retroactively accommodates the preceding narrative, giving imaginative endorsement to those details that fit with this view. Gulliver pays the price for tragic knowledge, experience exacts a penalty, not in this case death, but madness.

How consistent such a judgment is with the detail of the text is left to the reader's assessment of the argument of this study as a whole, and the fourth voyage in particular, which largely offers evidence for a "soft" school reading. James L. Clifford acknowledges various gradations between these schematic extremes.[1] Any work as complex as *Gulliver's Travels* is unlikely to offer such pat resolutions. Could it be said against the "soft" reading here that it possibly responds more to ideas than to imagination? The "hard" school cannot be complacently dismissed. There is indeed a nagging doubt about that final crazed image of Gulliver that must be confronted. The dialectic of the closing satirical frame will be analyzed as follows: Swift's final satirical strategy; the question of readership; and the synthesis of history, which offers a resolution of the critical polarity.

In figure 1, "The Dialectic of Gulliver's Travels," shown in chapter 5 of this volume, section 4 opposes the "madness, delusion, and falsity" of Gulliver with the "sanity, reality, and truth" of Swift. At this point the dialectic of the satirist is brought to a halt, but Swift has no control of the dialectic of history, which bears the significance of *Gulliver* forward to our own day. Gulliver is driven mad by misanthropic disillusion at the failure of his reformatory book of travels.

Given the details of his background as indicated in chapter 5 of this study, and given the social positioning of Gulliver hinted at thereafter, it is difficult to make a contemporary analogy. It should, however, be attempted, since most modern commentators underestimate Gulliver's social significance. From an American viewpoint, think of an Eastern Democrat reading an account of an Arkansas Republican Baptist who, after an enforced stay in California, has been converted to Zen Buddhism and returns home only to have his Good News rejected. That is more or less how an upper-class educated Tory gentleman would have seen Lemuel Gulliver, the Puritan converted to deistic rationalism.

Madness completes the process of Gulliver's social invalidation. By *social invalidation* is meant the way in which one group in society antipathetic to the views or lifestyle of another, usually less powerful group will evade direct debate by dismissing persons instead of arguing ideas. Thus at different times in the twentieth century homosexuals, women, blacks, Jews, and a variety of minor religious, racial, and ethnic groups have been dismissed out of hand simply because of their color, place of birth, or belief. Nothing they say could be of any value simply because of what they are. In a nutshell, so-called dissidents are proscribed rather than listened to. The proscribing power group crushes, laughs at, imprisons, murders those who will not conform to its ideology. One of the most notorious such situations in this century was the use of mental hospitals under Stalin to purge Marxist dissidents, religious nonconformists, or anyone who opposed the state. To dissent is to be mad. Swift's social invalidation of Gulliver is a dialectical sanction of his class ideology—in broad terms, his reactionary conservatism as against Gulliver's progressive nonconformist modernism. The situation of Swift and Gulliver is a fascinating inversion of the Stalinist gulag archipelago. Swift by the 1720s was the marginalized intellectual dissident, in effect, and Gulliver the representative of the growing mercantile power of nonconformity within Whiggism. Swift's satirical invalidation makes Gulliver mad amidst strange islands. If there is one word that comprehensively indicates what Gulliver represents, it is *modern,* and this is manifestly the case, even in the fourth voyage. There is a complex of meanings attached to the Houyhnhnms, not least being their *modernism*. As neo-Stoic Deists, that is what they amount to, and, consistent with the work as a whole, Gulliver as author is their fervent admirer.

The dialectic ceases at a point at which Swift's legitimation as successful satirist triumphs over Gulliver as failed reformist writer, the victim of his own pride. Swift invalidates actualities of his own world by making them ultimately ludicrous and dismissible in the figure of Gulliver. The ground is laid in parts I and II, in which the traveler undergoes a process of depersonalization from monster to vermin, until he actually experiences himself in a schizophrenic way: "I really began to imagine my self dwindled many Degrees below my usual size" (II.iii.99). Wherever Gulliver turns in part III he is faced with a sense of his moral, political, or intellectual inferiority. Swift's final omniscience as author expresses his ostensive omniscience as moral spokesman. Swift's omniscience is final because the dialectic ceases just at the point in the book where Gulliver's patent claims to personality and authorship are revealed as ludicrous.

The opening of the last chapter adopts the conventional claims of the travel writer's bona fides. Gulliver addresses the reader with assurances of simple authenticity, abjuring the fantastic, claiming, "I have not been so studious of Ornament as of Truth" (IV.xii.299). A crucial insistence is worth a longer quote: "I imposed on my self as a Maxim, never to be swerved from, that I would *strictly adhere to Truth;* neither indeed can I be ever under the least Temptation to vary from it, while I retain in my Mind the Lectures and Example of my noble Master, and the other illustrious *Houyhnhnms,* of whom I had so long the Honour to be an humble Hearer." He then slips in two lines of Latin: "*Nec si miserum Fortuna Sinonem / Finxit, vanum etiam, mendacemque improba finget.*" Paul Turner's edition offers this translation, from Virgil's *Aeneid* (ii.79–80): "nor, if cruel Fortune has made Sinon miserable, shall she also make him false and deceitful." Taken out of the Virgilian context, with Gulliver exchanged for Sinon, this statement seems to summarize the traveler's position of Houyhnhnm probity. While the quotation of Latin is somewhat problematic, since it is a rhetorical ornament Gulliver has just rejected and is at odds with the dissenting traveler's style, these objections are nothing to what the context reveals.

The speaker of these lines is Aeneas, repeating the words of Sinon, who mutilated himself to convince the Trojans that he had been badly treated by the Greeks. His ulterior motive was to persuade the Trojans to accept the placatory gift of the wooden horse. When the gift was duly admitted, Sinon released the hidden Greek soldiers and thus Troy fell. Aeneas is relating the events retrospectively by which his audience—and the readers of the *Aeneid*—knew that Sinon is a liar. Gulliver could not have chosen a worse quote in the whole of classical literature. Swift could not have chosen a more ironic couplet. Clearly the book *Gulliver's Travels* smuggles in the deceit and treachery of horse rationalism into Augustan London. To cap it all, as he did in his poem "A Description of a City Shower," Swift plays on the idea of London's old mythological name, Troy Novant, or New Troy, deriving from the supposed arrival of the fleeing Trojan Brut. The Latin quote is not identified as Virgil. At this point mutual identification between Swift and his educated, witty, superior audience takes place. Part of the satire lies in the corroboration of a readership's credentials in recognizing sophisticated elitism within a populist mode.

Pope's mock-heroic poem of 1728, *The Dunciad,* is the major early-eighteenth-century testament to the rise of what was called Grub Street. It was the combined London world of writers and bookseller-publisher-printers cashing in on increased literacy, cheaper paper, and an ever-increasing demand for novels, magazines, and newspapers—print of any kind, in fact, from cheap pamphlet chapbooks to Pope's Homer (subscription only, initially). Chapbooks were sold by chapmen like Autolycus in *The Winter's Tale* or from their place of publication, mostly London. Including a few cheap woodcuts, these brief stories purveyed romance, crime, religion, prophecy, dreams, folklore, sensation, and disaster, natural and spiritual. Even Sir John Mandeville's *Travels* persisted in an eleven-page eighteenth-century version. Summaries of *Moll Flanders* and *Robinson Crusoe* (in woodcuts) found their way into the chapbook trade.[2] At the other extreme were the beautiful and expensive folios of Pope's Homer. These were the termini of populist and aristocratic taste of the day. In between, toward the lower end romance and picaresque dominated, while at the educated heights were various editions of classical authors.

The coffeehouse and club culture of the London professions, aristocracy, literati, and hangers-on fostered an elitist readership whose watchword was "wit." Swift, Bolingbroke, and others founded the Tory "Brothers Club" as a counterpart to the Whig Kit-Cat Club, and in a letter Bolingbroke outlines the program as follows: "We shall begin to meet in a small number, and that will be composed of some who have wit and learning to recommend them."[3] Not the vulgar libertinism of the Restoration but the polished literary wit associated with Augustan urbanity sustained their meetings. The foundation of wit was knowledge of classical languages and literature. Popular literature required no learning. The word *vulgar* derives from *vulgus,* "the people." Swift considered Defoe a vulgarian writing for the inferior, relatively uneducated classes of society. The wit of *Gulliver's Travels* is to take a popular form, travel writing, and to combine it with an allusive, ironic mode, satire. Swift thereby achieved a populist success and created an elitist masterpiece, exactly as Ben Jonson had done with *Bartholomew Fair* (1614). The membership of the Scriblerus Club— Pope, Arbuthnot, Gay, Parnell, and Robert Harley, Earl of Oxford— typified those readers who could relish a range of ironic allusion. Meanwhile, those who delighted in *Robinson Crusoe* could thrill at Gulliver's adventures.

However much twentieth-century readers attempt to immerse themselves in the habits, mentality, and ethos of a past era, they remain twentieth-century readers. Conversely, the meaning of literary works considered of lasting importance is rarely confined to contemporary reference. History, like *meaning,* is dynamic and ceaseless, always providing new perspectives with each shift of culture. From a late-twentieth-century vantage point the "soft" and "hard" schools can, to some extent, be reconciled by the concept of satire, using madness as a process of social invalidation. If the "hard" school could forsake the insistence on the Houyhnhnms as offering an ideal and yet retain the sense of Gulliver's final predicament as going beyond the comic, then the above reading can accommodate both views—assuming that Swift is recognized as giving voice not to a set of absolute values but to a relative ideology of class and culture which was eventually resolved in the course of the eighteenth century by accommodation rather than conflict. Gulliver the individual may be alienated, but Swift's art as a kind of social exorcism of the body politic could not exorcise a whole entrepreneurial ethos whose utilitarian modernism, fired by the Protestant ethic, was to go beyond the ne plus ultra of class and land to create the new urban, commercial, and middle-class world that still, in large part, shapes our society.

Most English-speaking readers today belong to democratic societies. Presuppositions of democratic culture will partially determine interpretation. Egalitarianism upholds respect for the individual and the nature of difference in society. Class, color, and religious prejudice and discrimination are considered not merely unacceptable but evil. Built into the American constitution and British law are a number of democratic rights that are taken for granted. All of these democratic values were fought for against old and new social systems, from feudalism and absolutism to Communism and Fascism. In this egalitarian struggle, ordinary people are always the first victims of purges, war, disease, hunger, imprisonment, torture, rape, and brutality. Their names are lost, only the anonymity of suffering remains, and we are their heirs and beneficiaries.

Complementing democratic individualism, the horror of much of the twentieth century has taught a distrust of bureaucracy, political philosophies, and state power. Out of the idealistic aspirations of nineteenth-century Europe arose megalithic totalitarian dystopias that finally crumbled in their own rottenness: Nazi Germany, Fascist Italy, the USSR. Probably here lies the attraction of Houyhnhnm idealism for "hard" school critics, not so much its moral primitivism but its complete freedom from the bureaucratic and technocratic monstrousness of twentieth-century barbarism, if we ignore the final solution of the Yahoos. Ideas of the public hero always seem suspect, whereas the little man as victim is an inescapable fact. This, I feel, accounts for the underlying impulse of the "hard" school criticism of *Gulliver's Travels,* deriving from a tragic sense of Gulliver as victim, of humans and nature, of society and the elements, of criminals, of circumstance, of politics, of madness, and, finally, of satire. Eighteenth-century tourists visited Bedlam as a form of entertainment. Today mental disorder is treated with care and compassion, or at least most everyone would agree that that should be the case. Feeling and imagination incline us, as mutually vulnerable persons and readers, to respond sympathetically to Gulliver's predicament.

The enthronement of imagination at the end of the eighteenth century itself in part derived from the transformation of moral sympathy into psychological empathy, which went hand in hand with the development of the novel. Empathetic reading of realistic fiction enabled entry into another individual's experience within society. I put it that the "hard" school brings to the reading of *Gulliver* an empathetic response to feelings subtly different from the imagination needed to respond to fantastic events and intellectual "entertainment." Swift's beliefs, invention, and humor were quite alien to the benevolist philosophy that triumphed. Sensibility, sentiment, and feeling ran deep, affecting individuals and society in ramified ways. Dr. Johnson set out to imitate the corrosive vehemence of Juvenal's Tenth Satire in "The Vanity of Human Wishes" and wrote an elegy on man, whatever his status, high or low, as more sinned against than sinning. Caught in a web of inscrutable but active powers beyond the individual will, the human being was always ultimately the victim of physical, metaphysical, or social forces. Even pride, like Gulliver's, becomes an externalized agent. In this respect Dr. Johnson anticipates Kafka as much as he looks back to Juvenal. In the last twenty years a new literature of the fantastic has arisen in such authors as Gabriel García Márquez, Gunther Grass, and Salman Rushdie, who write unrestrained by the conventions of realism. It is hoped that this literature will attract new readers looking back to *Gulliver's Travels* as forebear to find that, more than he anticipated, Swift is still capable of vexing the world.

Notes and References

The following works are cited here in full at first reference; thereafter they are cited parenthetically in the text.

Chapter 1

1. Kathleen Williams, ed., *Swift: The Critical Heritage* (London: Routledge and Kegan Paul, 1970), 61–62.

2. See Percy G. Adams, *Travelers and Travel Liars 1660–1800* (Berkeley and Los Angeles: University of California Press, 1962).

3. See Rudolf Wittkower, "Marvels of the East," *Journal of the Warburg and Courtauld Institute* 5 (1942): 159–97.

4. *The Book of Ser Marco Polo,* 3d ed., trans. and ed. Sir Henry Yule (London: John Murray, 1926), 2:412.

5. J. H. Parry, *The Age of Reconnaissance* (New York: Mentor, 1963).

6. See G. R. Crone, *Maps and Their Makers* (London: Hutchinson, 1953).

7. Arthur Sherbo, "Swift and Travel Literature," *Modern Language Studies* 9 (1979): 114–27.

8. Arthur E. Case, "The Geography and Chronology of *Gulliver's Travels,*" in *Four Essays on "Gulliver's Travels"* (Gloucester, Mass.: Peter Smith, 1958), 50–68.

9. William A. Eddy, *"Gulliver's Travels": A Critical Study* (Princeton: Princeton University Press, 1923).

10. See Geoffroy Atkinson, *The Extraordinary Voyage in French Literature before 1700* (New York: Columbia University Press, 1920).

Chapter 3

1. For the balance of this chapter, eighteenth- and nineteenth-century references up to Hazlitt are from Kathleen Williams, ed., *Swift: The Critical Heritage* (London: Routledge and Kegan Paul, 1970). Later nineteenth-centu-

ry references and twentieth-century references through 1963 are from Milton Voigt, *Swift and the Twentieth Century* (Detroit: University of Michigan Press, 1964). References published since 1964 are from Brian Tippett, *"Gulliver's Travels": "The Critics Debate"* (Houndmills and London: Macmillan, 1989), unless otherwise noted.

2. Norman O. Brown, *Life against Death: The Psychoanalytical Meaning of History* (London: Sphere Books, 1970). See "The Excremental Vision," chapter 13, 163–81.

3. J. Churton Collins, *Jonathan Swift: A Biographical and Critical Study* (London, 1893), 230; R. M. Frye, "Swift's Yahoos and the Christian Symbols of Sin," *Journal of the History of Ideas* 15 (1954): 201–17.

4. Carole Fabricant, *Swift's Landscape* (Baltimore: Johns Hopkins University Press, 1982).

5. Irvin Ehrenpreis, *Swift: The Man, His Works, and the Age.* 3 vols. (London: Methuen, 1962, 1967, 1983); Louis A. Landa, *Swift and the Church of Ireland* (Oxford: Clarendon Press, 1959).

6. Sir Charles Firth, "The Political Significance of *Gulliver's Travels*," reprinted in *Essays Historical and Literary* (Oxford: Clarendon Press, 1938): 210–41; Arthur E. Case, *Four Essays on "Gulliver's Travels"* (Gloucester, Mass: Peter Smith, 1978); W. A. Speck, *Society and Literature in England 1700–1760* (Dublin: Gill and Macmillan, 1983); J. A. Downie, *Jonathan Swift: Political Writer* (London, Boston, and Henley: Routledge and Kegan Paul, 1984); F. P. Lock, *The Politics of "Gulliver's Travels"* (Oxford: Clarendon Press, 1980).

7. See Voigt, *Swift and the Twentieth Century,* 157.

8. James L. Clifford, "Gulliver's Fourth Voyage: 'Hard' and 'Soft' Schools of Interpretation," in *Quick Springs of Sense: Studies in the Eighteenth Century,* ed. Larry S. Champion (Athens: University of Georgia Press, 1974), 33–49.

9. C. J. Rawson, *Gulliver and the Gentle Reader* (London and Boston: Routledge and Kegan Paul, 1973).

10. W. B. Carnochan, *Lemuel Gulliver's Mirror for Man* (Berkeley and Los Angeles: University of California Press, 1968).

11. Everett Zimmerman, *Swift's Narrative Satires* (Ithaca and London: Cornell University Press, 1983); Nigel Wood, *Swift* (Brighton: Harvester, 1986).

12. Alain Bony, "Call Me Gulliver," *Poetique* 14 (1973): 197–209.

13. Terry Castle, "Why the Houyhnhnms Don't Write: Swift, Satire and the Fear of the Text," *Essays in Literature* 7 (1980): 31–44; Grant Holly, "Travel and Translation: Textuality in *Gulliver's Travels*," *Criticism* 21 (1979): 134–52.

14. See *Gulliver's Travels,* ed. Christopher Fox (Boston: Bedford Books of St. Martin's Press, 1994).

Notes and References

15. Edward Said, *The World, the Text, and the Critic* (London: Vintage, 1984); Bertrand Goldgar, *Walpole among the Wits* (Lincoln: University of Nebraska Press, 1976); Speck, *Society and Literature* (previously cited).

Chapter 4

1. M. M. Knappen, *Tudor Puritanism* (Chicago and London: University of Chicago Press, 1939), 330.

2. E. A. Block, "Lemuel Gulliver: Middle-Class Englishman," *English Language Notes* 68 (1933): 474–77.

Chapter 5

1. Sir Charles Firth, "The Political Significance of *Gulliver's Travels*," reprinted in *Essays Historical and Literary* (Oxford: Clarendon Press, 1938): 210–41.

2. W. A. Speck, *Swift* (London: Evans Bros., 1969), 105–13.

3. J. A. Downie, "Political Characterization in *Gulliver's Travels*," *Yearbook of English Studies* 7 (1977): 108–20; and F. P. Lock, *The Politics of "Gulliver's Travels"* (Oxford: Clarendon Press, 1980).

4. Denis Donoghue, ed., *Jonathan Swift* (Harmondsworth: Penguin Books, 1971), 135, quoting from W. B. Yeats's introduction to *The Words upon the Window-Pane* (1934).

Chapter 6

1. Marjorie Nicolson, "The Microscope and the English Imagination," in *Science and Imagination* (Ithaca, N.Y.: Great Seal Books, Cornell University Press, 1962), 155–207. For the scientific background I am indebted to this and other articles listed below.

2. Clive T. Probyn, *Jonathan Swift: The Contemporary Background* (Manchester: Manchester University Press, 1978), 189.

Chapter 7

1. Marjorie Nicolson and Nora M. Mohler, "Swift's 'Flying Island' in the Voyage to Laputa," *Annals of Science* 2 (1937): 421.

2. For details concerning Irish history I am indebted to the following study: Oliver W. Ferguson, *Jonathan Swift and Ireland* (Urbana: University of Illinois Press, 1962).

Chapter 8

1. The best account of the use of experimental science remains Richard Foster Jones's *Ancients and Moderns,* 2d ed. (Berkeley and Los Angeles: University of California Press, 1961).

2. David Ogg, *England in the Reign of Charles II* (Oxford: Oxford University Press, 1963), 722.

3. Marjorie Nicolson and Nora M. Mohler, "The Scientific Background of Swift's Voyage to Laputa," *Annals of Science* 2 (1937): 299–334.

4. *Journal to Stella* (Oxford: Clarendon Press, 1948) I, 122.

5. Hans Baron, "The *Querelle* of the Ancients and Moderns as a Problem for Renaissance Scholarship," *Journal of the History of Ideas* 20 (1959): 3–22. The most thoroughgoing study of the English "Battle" to date is Joseph M. Levine, *The Battle of the Books* (Ithaca and London: Cornell University Press, 1991).

6. For the place of the sextumvirate in Swift's writings, see M. M. Kelsall, "Iterum Houyhnhnm: Swift's Sextumvirate and the Horses," *Essays in Criticism* 19 (1969): 35–45.

Chapter 9

1. See George Boas, *The Happy Beast* (New York: Octagon Books, 1966).

2. See David Kunzle, "World Upside Down: The Iconography of a European Broadsheet," in *The Reversible World: Symbolic Inversion in Art and Society,* ed. Barbara Babcock (Ithaca and London: Cornell University Press, 1978), 39–94.

3. For a fuller discussion of utopian backgrounds see Brian Vickers, "The Satiric Structure of *Gulliver's Travels* and More's *Utopia*," in *The World of Jonathan Swift,* ed. Brian Vickers (Oxford: Blackwell, 1968), 233–57; Ian Higgins, "Swift and Sparta: The Nostalgia of *Gulliver's Travels*," *Modern Language Review* 78 (1983): 513–31; and John F. Reichert, "Plato, Swift, and the Houyhnhnms," *Philological Quarterly* 47 (1968): 179–92.

4. See Irvin Ehrenpreis, *The Personality of Jonathan Swift* (London: Methuen, 1958); and Kathleen Williams, *Jonathan Swift and the Age of Compromise* (Lawrence: University of Kansas Press, 1967).

5. See J. J. McManmon, "The Problem of a Religious Interpretation of Gulliver's Fourth Voyage," *Journal of the History of Ideas* 27 (1966): 59–72.

6. See G. R. Cragg, *Reason and Authority in the Eighteenth Century* (Cambridge: Cambridge University Press, 1964), 78–83.

7. See Ronald Knowles, "Swift's Yahoos, Aphrodite, and Hyginus Fabula CCXX," *English Language Notes* 31 (1993): 44–45.

8. Steward Lacasce, "The Fall of Gulliver's Master," *Essays in Criticism* 20 (1970): 327–33.

9. Ludwig Wittgenstein, *The Tractatus Logico-Philosophicus* (London: Routledge and Kegan Paul, 1961), 115, proposition 5.6.

10. R. S. Crane. "The Houyhnhnms, the Yahoos, and the History of Ideas," in *Reason and Imagination,* ed. J. A. Mazzeo (London: Routledge and Kegan Paul, 1962).

Notes and References

Chapter 10

1. A useful update on Clifford's review may be found in Richard H. Rodino, *Swift Studies 1965–1980: An Annotated Bibliography* (New York and London: Garland, 1984), xxx–xxxvi.

2. See John Ashton, *Chap-Books of the Eighteenth Century* (London: Chatto and Windus, 1882).

3. Charles Kerby-Miller, ed., *The Memoirs of the Extraordinary Life, Works, and Discoveries of Martinus Scriblerus* (New York and Oxford: Oxford University Press, 1988), 5.

Bibliography

Primary Works

In addition to the edition of *Gulliver's Travels* by Paul Turner, *The Prose Works* edited by Herbert Davis, and the *Correspondence* edited by Harold Williams—all cited at the beginning of this volume in "Note on the References and Acknowledgments"—the Oxford Authors series' *Jonathan Swift,* edited by Angus Ross and David Woolley (Oxford: Oxford University Press, 1984), offers an excellent selection of Swift's writings (excluding *Gulliver*). Though slightly older, the following remains useful: R. A. Greenberg and W. B. Piper, eds., *The Writings of Jonathan Swift* (New York and London: W. W. Norton, 1973). Christopher Fox's edition of *Gulliver's Travels* in the Case Studies in Contemporary Criticism series published by Bedford Books of St. Martin's Press (Boston, 1994) is outstanding. Pat Rogers, ed., *The Complete Poems* (Harmondsworth: Penguin, 1983), is profusely annotated.

Secondary Works

Biography

Downie, J. A. *Jonathan Swift: Political Writer.* London, Boston, and Henley: Routledge and Kegan Paul, 1984. A superbly balanced study of Swift's life, politics, and writing. Excellent for introductory and continuing study.

Ehrenpreis, Irvin. *Swift: The Man, His Works, and the Age.* Vol. 1, *Mr. Swift and His Contemporaries,* vol. 2, *Dr. Swift,* vol. 3, *Dean Swift.* London: Methuen, 1962, 1967, 1983. The authoritative biography.

Nokes, David. *Jonathan Swift: A Hypocrite Reversed*. Oxford: Oxford University Press, 1985. A prize-winning work.

Critical Overviews

Clifford, James L. "Gulliver's Fourth Voyage. 'Hard' and 'Soft' Schools of Interpretation." In *Quick Springs of Sense: Studies in the Eighteenth Century,* edited by Larry S. Champion. Athens: University of Georgia Press, 1974. Still the best way into the continuing debate.

Clubb, Merrel D. "The Criticism of Gulliver's 'Voyage to the Houyhnhnms,' 1726–1914." In *Stanford Studies in Language and Literature,* edited by Hardin Craig. Stanford, Calif.: Stanford University Press, 1941. Presents a critical synthesis, in effect, of materials collected by Kathleen Williams, below.

Donoghue, Denis, ed. *Jonathan Swift*. Harmondsworth: Penguin, 1971. A generous critical anthology on particular works and "general estimates."

Rodino, Richard H. *Swift Studies, 1965–1980.* See below under Bibliographies. The introduction contains a useful update on Clifford.

Tippett, Brian. *"Gulliver's Travels."* Houndmills and London: Macmillan, 1989. One of "The Critics Debate" series. An invaluable "survey" section.

Voigt, Milton. *Swift and the Twentieth Century.* Detroit: Wayne State University Press, 1964. Still useful, not least for the summaries on Freudianism.

Williams, Kathleen, ed. *Swift: The Critical Heritage.* London: Routledge and Kegan Paul, 1970. Collects comment from contemporaries up to the early nineteenth century.

Other Books Consulted

Adams, Percy G. *Travelers and Travel Liars, 1660–1800.* Berkeley and Los Angeles: University of California Press, 1962. Extremely useful background material.

Ashton, John. *Chap-Books of the Eighteenth Century.* London: Chatto and Windus, 1882. Many examples of populist reading.

Atkinson, Geoffroy. *The Extraordinary Voyage in French Literature before 1700.* New York: Columbia University Press, 1920. Good account of deist utopias.

Babcock, Barbara, ed. *The Reversible World: Symbolic Inversion in Art and Society.* Ithaca and London: Cornell University Press, 1978. See David Kunzle, "World Upside Down: The Iconography of a European Broadsheet." This material suggests an added dimension to the Houyhnhnms.

Bellamy, Liz. *Jonathan Swift's "Gulliver's Travels."* New York and London: Harvester Wheatsheaf, 1992. Offers an ideological reading of Swift's politics.

Bibliography

Boas, George. *The Happy Beast*. New York: Octagon Books, 1966. Seventeenth-century theriophily in reaction to Montaigne.

Brown, Norman O. *Life against Death: The Psychoanalytical Meaning of History*. London: Sphere Books, 1970. "The Excremental Vision" explores Swift as anal seer.

Carnochan, W. B. *Lemuel Gulliver's Mirror for Man*. Berkeley and Los Angeles: University of California Press, 1968. Philosophical background.

Case, Arthur E. *Four Essays on "Gulliver's Travels."* Gloucester, Mass.: Peter Smith, 1978. An important essay on geography.

Cragg, G. R. *Reason and Authority in the Eighteenth Century*. Cambridge: Cambridge University Press, 1964. A leading authority on the English Church. Excellent discussion of Deism.

Crone, G. R. *Maps and Their Makers*. London: Hutchinson, 1953. A straightforward account of the subject, concisely put.

Dampier, William. *A New Voyage round the World*. London: Argonaut Press, 1927. Worth sampling to compare Gulliver's style.

Eddy, William A. *"Gulliver's Travels": A Critical Study*. Princeton: Princeton University Press, 1923. A still valuable sourcebook despite poor production and design and a nineteenth-century response to the fourth voyage.

Ehrenpreis, Irvin. *The Personality of Jonathan Swift*. London: Methuen, 1958. A partly deist reading of the Houyhnhnms.

Erskine-Hill, Howard. *"Gulliver's Travels."* Cambridge: Cambridge University Press, 1993. Challenges deist readings of part IV. Gives an interesting sketch of the literary legacy of *Gulliver*.

Fabricant, Carole. *Swift's Landscape*. Baltimore: Johns Hopkins University Press, 1982. An impressively researched study of both town and country environment.

Ferguson, Oliver W. *Jonathan Swift and Ireland*. Urbana: University of Illinois Press, 1962. Assembles all the relevant historical materials.

Firth, Sir Charles. *Essays Historical and Literary*. Oxford: Clarendon Press, 1938. Includes "The Political Significance of *Gulliver's Travels*." Influential but dated. (Reprinted in Gravil.)

Goldgar, Bertrand. *Walpole among the Wits*. Lincoln: University of Nebraska Press, 1976. Topical background on the 1720s.

Griffin, Dustin H. *Satires against Man: The Poems of Rochester*. Berkeley, Los Angeles, and London: University of California Press, 1973. Discusses French tradition of universalizing satire.

Hammond, Brean. *"Gulliver's Travels."* Milton Keynes and Philadelphia: Open University Press, 1988. Challenging, lively interrogative style.

Jones, Richard Foster. *Ancients and Moderns*. Berkeley and Los Angeles: University of California Press, 1961. The scientific background, packed with research.

Kerby-Miller, Charles, ed. *The Memoirs of the Extraordinary Life, Works, and Discoveries of Martinus Scriblerus.* New York and Oxford: Oxford University Press, 1988. The generous introduction gives a good idea of the clubby elitist milieu of Georgian London.

Knappen, M. M. *Tudor Puritanism.* Chicago and London: University of Chicago Press, 1939. The contexts of Gulliver's forebears.

Landa, Louis A. *Swift and the Church of Ireland.* Oxford: Clarendon Press, 1959. The authoritative scholar on the subject.

Levine, Joseph M. *"The Battle of the Books": History and Literature in the Augustan Age.* Ithaca and London: Cornell University Press, 1991. The fullest study to date of the literary, historicist, and antiquarian issues.

Lock, F. P. *The Politics of "Gulliver's Travels."* Oxford: Clarendon Press, 1980. Argues for Swift as concerned not just with topical affairs but with Europe past and present.

Mazzeo, J. A. *Reason and Imagination.* London: Routledge and Kegan Paul, 1962. See R. S. Crane, "The Houyhnhnms, the Yahoos, and the History of Ideas." Overrated, question-begging, and paradoxical, this work does nevertheless add one crucial fact to interpretation of the Houyhnhnms—the function of the example of *equus* in logic textbooks.

Nicolson, Marjorie. *Science and Imagination.* Ithaca: Cornell University Press, 1956. Indispensable for the essay "The Microscope and the English Imagination."

Ogg, David. *England in the Reign of Charles II.* Oxford: Oxford University Press, 1963. Covers all areas of life for Swift's seventeenth-century background.

Parry, J. H. *The Age of Reconnaissance.* New York: Mentor, 1963. Surveys maritime business and seamanship, the discoveries, and the colonial legacy.

Probyn, Clive T. *Gulliver's Travels.* Harmondsworth: Penguin, 1987. Good introduction by way of Swift's other prose satires.

———. *Jonathan Swift: The Contemporary Background.* Manchester: Manchester University Press, 1978. An excellent collection of gobbets from contemporary sources with separate, valuable introductions.

Rawson, C. J. *Gulliver and the Gentle Reader.* London and Boston: Routledge and Kegan Paul, 1973. Comparative discussion of Swift and twentieth-century writing.

Reilly, Edward J. *Approaches to Teaching "Gulliver's Travels."* New York: Modern Language Association, 1988. From an excellent series for students and teachers alike.

Said, Edward. *The World, the Text, and the Critic.* London: Vintage, 1984. Challenges poststructuralist ahistoricism.

Bibliography

Schakel, Peter J. *Critical Approaches to Teaching Swift.* New York: AMS Press, 1992. See Richard H. Rodino, "The Study of *Gulliver's Travels* Past and Future."

Smith, Frederick N. *The Genres of "Gulliver's Travels."* Newark: University of Delaware Press, 1990. Chapters on travel, the picaresque, children's literature, science fiction, illustration.

Speck, W. A. *Society and Literature in England, 1700–1760.* Dublin: Gill and Macmillan, 1983. Good on Tory satire of the 1720s.

Williams, Kathleen. *Jonathan Swift and the Age of Compromise.* Lawrence: University of Kansas Press, 1967. An influential study still worth turning back to.

Wood, Nigel. *Swift.* Brighton: Harvester, 1986. Modern theoretical readings.

Yule, Sir Henry, trans. and ed. *The Book of Ser Marco Polo.* London: John Murray, 1926. One of the great sourcebooks for Renaissance explorers, mapmakers, and fantasists.

Zimmerman, Everett. *Swift's Narrative Satires.* Ithaca and London: Cornell University Press, 1983. Considers *A Tale of a Tub* and *Gulliver* in relation to textuality and epistemology.

Articles

Baron, Hans. "The *Querelle* of the Ancients and Moderns as a Problem for Renaissance Scholarship." *Journal of the History of Ideas* 20 (1959): 3–22. The continental historical background for *The Battle of the Books.*

Block, Edward A. "Lemuel Gulliver: Middle-Class Englishman." *Modern Language Notes* 68 (1953): 474–77. A note that has helped perpetuate the notion of Gulliver's averageness and universality.

Bony, Alain. "Call Me Gulliver." *Poetique* 14 (1973): 197–209. Postmodernist study of Gulliver as a construction of the reader. See Castle and Holly.

Brady, Frank. "Vexations and Diversions: Three Problems in *Gulliver's Travels.*" *Modern Philology* 75 (1977–78): 346–67. Analyzes the methodology, or lack of it, of critical approaches.

Carnochan, W. B. "Some Roles of Lemuel Gulliver." *Texas Studies in Language and Literature* 5 (1964): 520–29. Gulliver as satirist-anatomist, court fool, victim, etc. A good antidote for naturalistic readings.

Castle, Terry. "Why the Houyhnhnms Don't Write: Swift, Satire, and the Fear of the Text." *Essays in Literature* 7 (1980): 31–44. A postmodernist study of textuality. See Bony and Holly.

Champion, Larry S. "Gulliver's Voyages: The Framing Events as a Guide to Interpretation." *Texas Studies in Language and Literature* 10 (1969): 529–36. Analyzes Swift's careful design and overall patterning.

GULLIVER'S TRAVELS

Clifford, James L. "Gulliver's Fourth Voyage: 'Hard' and 'Soft' Schools of Interpretation." See under Critical Overviews, above.

Downie, J. H. "Political Characterization in *Gulliver's Travels*." *Yearbook of English Studies* 7 (1977): 108–20. Reexamines topical specificity, but is unwilling to concede overall generality.

Frye, R. M. "Swift's Yahoos and the Christian Symbols of Sin." *Journal of the History of Ideas* 15 (1954): 201–17. A valuable assessment of the theological contribution to the depiction of the Yahoos. (Reprinted in Foster.)

Gill, James E. "Beast over Man: Theriophilic Paradox in Gulliver's 'Voyage to the Country of the Houyhnhnms.'" *Studies in Philology* 67 (1970): 532–49. An important study of a somewhat neglected but vital aspect. See George Boas above.

Higgins, Ian. "Swift and Sparta: The Nostalgia of *Gulliver's Travels*." *Modern Language Review* 78 (1983): 513–31. The best examination of the topic, raising problems for "soft" school readings of part IV.

Holly, Grant. "Travel and Translation: Textuality in *Gulliver's Travels*." *Criticism* 21 (1979): 134–52. Another postmodernist study of "presence" in the text. See Castle and Bony.

Kelsall, M. M. "Iterum Houyhnhnm: Swift's Sextumvirate and the Horses." *Essays in Criticism* 19 (1969): 44–55. Offers evidence of the sextumvirate in *Gulliver* and elsewhere in Swift's writings for a "hard" school interpretation. (Reprinted in Gravil.)

Knowles, Ronald. "Swift's Yahoos, Aphrodite, and Hyginus Fabula CCXX." *English Language Notes* 31 (1993): 44–45. A classical, not biblical, source for the Yahoos.

Lacasce, Steward. "The Fall of Gulliver's Master." *Essays in Criticism* 20 (1970): 327–33. Gulliver as the serpent bringing fallen knowledge to the Houyhnhnm Eden.

McManmon, J. J. "The Problem of a Religious Interpretation of Gulliver's Fourth Voyage." *Journal of the History of Ideas* 17 (1966): 59–72. Denies any internal evidence without reference to immediate external social and polemical circumstances.

Nicolson, Marjorie, and Nora M. Mohler. "The Scientific Background of Swift's 'Voyage to Laputa.'" *Annals of Science* 2 (1937): 299–334. Ground-breaking and indispensable. The background of the Grand Academy of Lagado. (Reprinted in Jeffares and in Nicolson's *Science and Imagination*.)

———. "Swift's 'Flying Island' in the 'Voyage to Laputa.'" *Annals of Science* 2 (1937): 405–30. Flight in science and fantasy. (Reprinted in Nicolson's *Science and Imagination*.)

Reichart, John F. "Plato, Swift, and the Houyhnhnms." *Philological Quarterly* 47 (1968): 179–92. Convincing argument for a strong Socratic element. See Kelsall above.

160

Bibliography

Ross, John F. "The Final Comedy of Lemuel Gulliver." *Studies in the Comic.* University of California Publications in English 8, no. 2 (1941): 175–96. Virtually began the "soft" school approach. (Reprinted in Foster, Gravil, and Tuveson.)

Sherbo, Arthur. "Swift and Travel Literature." *Modern Language Studies* 9 (1979): 114–27. Richly researched—essential reading.

Stone, Edward. "Swift and the Horses: Misanthropy or Comedy?" *Modern Language Quarterly* 10 (1949): 367–76. An early "soft" reading.

Vickers, Brian. "The Satiric Structure of *Gulliver's Travels* and More's *Utopia.*" (In his *The World of Jonathan Swift,* cited under Collections of Articles, below.) An important analysis of Swift's debt to a member of the sextumvirate. See Reichart and Kelsall.

Wedel, T. O. "On the Philosophical Background of *Gulliver's Travels.*" *Studies in Philology* 23 (1926): 442–50. Hobbes versus Locke in part IV. Still remains a valuable study. (Reprinted in Foster and Gravil.)

White, John H. "Swift's Trojan Horses: 'Reasoning but to Err.'" *English Language Notes* 3 (1966): 185–94. On inconsistency and illogicality in part IV.

Wittkower, Rudolf. "Marvels of the East." *Journal of the Warburg and Courtauld Institute* 5 (1942): 159–97. An illustrated discussion of the sources and transmission of the fantastic in European culture.

Yeomans, W. E. "The Houyhnhnm as Menippean Horse." *College English* 27 (1966): 449–54. Background of classical satire. (Reprinted in Gravil.)

Collections of Articles

Foster, Milton P., ed. *A Casebook on Gulliver among the Houyhnhnms.* New York: Thomas Y. Crowell, 1961.

Gravil, Richard, ed. *Swift: "Gulliver's Travels."* London: Macmillan, 1974.

Jeffares, A. Norman, ed. *Fair Liberty Was All His Cry.* London: Macmillan, 1967.

Tuveson, Ernest, ed. *Swift: A Collection of Critical Essays.* Englewood Cliffs, N.J.: Prentice-Hall, 1964.

Vickers, Brian, ed. *The World of Jonathan Swift.* Oxford: Blackwell, 1968.

Bibliographies

Rodino, Richard H., ed. *Swift Studies 1965–1980: An Annotated Bibliography.* New York and London: Garland, 1984. For more recent publications consult *The Year's Work in English Studies* and *The Modern Language Association Annual Bibliography.*

Teerink, H. *A Bibliography of the Writings of Jonathan Swift.* Edited by Arthur H. Scouten. Philadelphia: University of Pennsylvania Press, 1963. The authoritative reference work.

Index

Index

Index

Pascal, Blaise, 78, 111
Paul, St.: Ephesians, 114–15, 128
Pelagius, 25
Persius: *Satire II*, 51
Phalaris, 103
Philosophical Transactions, 102,
    103, 104. *See also* Royal
    Society
Pindar, 88
Plato: *Republic*, 17, 21, 22, 71, 81,
    126–27, 128, 100, 119
Pliny the Elder: *Natural History*, 7,
    9, 12, 59
Plutarch: *Life of Lycurgus*, 17, 71,
    118, 128; *Gryllus*, 24, 53
Polo, Marco: *The Book of Ser Marco
    Polo*; 7, 8, 10
Pope, Alexander, 33, 47, 63, 136,
    137; *The Dunciad*, 29, 145;
    An Essay on Man, 80; "An
    Epistle to Burlington," 99
portolan maps, 9
Probyn, Clive T., 81
Proverbs, 48
Psalmanazar, George: *An Historical
    and Geographical Description
    of Formosa*, 5–6; *Memoirs*, 6
Ptolemy: *Geography*, 9
Purchas, Samuel: *Hakluytus
    Posthumous*, 13, 14
Puritans, 48, 50, 51, 54–55, 58, 59
Pyrrho, 60

Rabelais, François, 18, 37, 103,
    104–5
Ramus, Petrus, 110
Rawson, C. J., 42
reason, 22–23, 61; and clothing,
    117–20; and dystopia,
    131–38; and the horse utopia,
    126–30; and theriophily,
    120–22
Regnier, Mathurin, 60
Richardson, Samuel: *Clarissa*, 34, 37

Royal Academy of Music, 89
Royal Society, 12, 61–62, 76, 77,
    81, 88, 90, 91, 99, 100–104,
    106, 112
Rushdie, Salman, 148

Said, Edward, 42
St. John, Henry, 28, 68–69, 129,
    146
satire: and dialectical irony, 52–53,
    57–59, 87, 121, 124, 140–41,
    144; and ideology, 142–43;
    and literalization of the
    metaphorical, 64, 89; and the
    logic of absurdity, 64, 111;
    and the mask-persona, 41, 51,
    52; and satirist as moral
    anatomist, 76; and *satura lanx*,
    86, 91–97. *See also* Horace,
    Lucian, Juvenal, Varro
Saussure, Ferdinand de, 42
Scott, Sir Walter, 37
Scotus, Duns, 110
Scriblerus Club, 59, 63, 146
Shadwell, Thomas: *The Virtuoso*,
    77
Shaftesbury, first Earl of, 27
Shaftesbury, third Earl of:
    Characteristics, 25, 37
Shakespeare, William, 37, 108; *King
    Lear*, 121; *The Winter's Tale*,
    145
Sherbo, Arthur, 13, 14
Sheridan, Thomas, 35–36, 37
Shklovskii, Viktor, 36
Sidney, Algernon, 111
Solzhenitzyn, Alexander, 84
Speck, W. A., 39, 42, 55, 69
Sprat, Thomas, *The History of the
    Royal Society*, 77, 101
Steele, Richard: *The Tatler*, 78
Stella (Hester Johnson), 76
Sterne, Laurence, 18
Stevens, Wallace, 42

Index

The Author

After receiving a first-class English honors degree from University College, Swansea, Ronald Knowles proceeded to graduate study at the Warburg Institute and Birkbeck College, University of London. He has taught all areas of English literature at the University of Reading since 1971, specializing in the early modern period and twentieth-century drama. His publications include a study of John Ogilby's festival for the Restoration of Charles II; the book *Henry IV, Parts One and Two;* and two books on the work of Harold Pinter. He is associate editor in Britain of the *Pinter Review.* Currently, he is editing the volume *Shakespeare, Carnival, and Society* and the text of Shakespeare's *Henry VI, Part Two.*

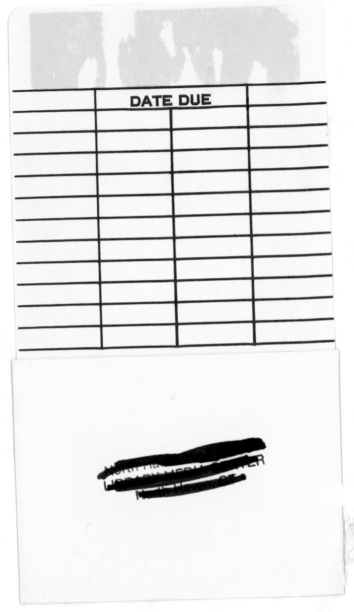

DATE DUE